Praise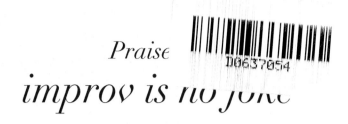

improv is no joke

"Keep it up...You are making a difference in people's lives..."

—Laimon Godel, CPA
CGMA at LW Godel, Jr. CPA, PC

"From the opening passage, I could tell *Improv is No Joke* was a different kind of book. The level of personal sharing from 'The Accidental Accountant™' is unlike any other book written by a bean counter! Peter Margaritis shares insights gained from a wide variety of careers and other pursuits many of us will never have the opportunity to experience ourselves. The lessons are accessible and immediately useful to anyone looking to improve their relationships, both personal and professional. It's the kind of information that can help anyone at any stage of career or season in life grow and prosper."

—John F Kelley
Vice President and Chief People Officer, White Castle Management, Co.

"Does *Improv is No Joke* deliver? Yes, and it will change the way you listen to your own inner voice on the path to a truly authentic expression of your strengths."

—Jamie Richardson
Vice President, White Castle Management, Co.

"I'm convinced...*Improv is No Joke*, Peter's insightful new book is written with humility, humor, and homespun wisdom. His premise is that one can find greater success in career and personal life by embracing and adapting the principles of improvisation. Through personal stories and anecdotes, he connects key improv skills such as 'parking your agenda' and responding with 'yes, and...' with personal and professional applications. The topics are broad and varied, but well integrated and include an improv look at everything from stress and risk taking to leadership and creativity. This book is a fun ride and reads like a letter from your favorite uncle. Before it's over you will have a smile on your face and a new ways to respond and adapt to life's challenges."

—Dr. Jay B. Young
Associate Professor, Ohio Dominican University

"Pete is a terrifically funny and relevant speaker and coach. You find yourself having so much fun you don't even realize you're learning so much along the way! I highly recommend using him to educate your employee base on a broad range of managerial skills while accomplishing some true team building."

—Tammy Dosch
CFO, Capital Square, Ltd.

"Peter was an outstanding speaker with a creative and very personal approach to leadership. Peter's unique message demonstrated that the principles of improvisational comedy are the same principles of an effective leader. Our staff team and our member leaders are implementing 'yes, and…' into our conversations, and it's making a positive difference."

—Stephanie Peters
CEO and president
Virginia Society of CPAs

"The passion and commitment you have for your business definitely shows through. It's obvious you take pride in the development and refinement of the content."

—Steven Dezenzo,
Manager, Finance & Accounting,
FedEx Custom Critical

"Peter is a CPA who sees the world creatively. Peter is a top-rated instructor and a thought leader with the Business Learning Institute who can help accounting professionals with essential business success skills to excel in today's rapidly changing business environment."

—Laura Dorsey-Shaner

Manager, BLI Key Accounts & Operations

"His ability to have fun and add humor to the subject is what made him night and day different than many other speakers. I highly recommend Peter if you are looking for someone to come and present a presentation for CPE opportunities or motivational team building."

—Keith O. Wilson, CPA, CFE, CGMA

Fraud Examiner, Bridgestone Americas, Inc.

"Peter Margaritis' presentation *Embrace Your Inner Superhero* was dynamic and passionate! Peter's experience and knowledge in the accounting industry drew me in and kept the audience interested and involved. For me, the presentation was interactive and thought provoking. Thanks, Peter."

—Sarah Galley, SPHR

Firm Administrator, Pohlman & Talmage CPAs, Inc.

"Peter spoke at our Association for Accounting Administration Ohio Chapter meeting. Peter's use of humor and interactive exercises helped us better understand the thought processes of CPAs. Peter provided communication tools to us to use to improve our communication with others and to also alleviate stress in our daily lives. The session wasn't over when Peter's presentation was finished. Attendees of the meeting gathered around him for some more gems of information! If you are in need of a speaker who can unleash your 'Superhero,' be sure to contact Peter."

—Marla Martin
Firm Administrator, Weber O'Brien Ltd.

"Pete is an engaging speaker with energy and keeps things interesting **and makes you laugh.** Pete has a good presentation style and **helps learning by telling real-life stories.** It is the real-life stories which drive the points home and greatly assist in helping attendees **retain the information."**

—*Seminar evaluation summary from an attendee at the Washington Society of CPAs on 12/11/14*

improv
is
no joke

Embrace
Yes And

improv
is
no joke

Using Improvisation *to*

Create Positive Results

in Leadership *and* Life

Peter A. Margaritis, CPA

Foreword by J. Clarke Price, FASAE, CAE

Published by Advantage, Charleston, South Carolina.
Member of Advantage Media Group.

ADVANTAGE is a registered trademark and the Advantage colophon is a trademark of Advantage Media Group, Inc.

Printed in the United States of America.

ISBN: 978-159932-541-5
LCCN: 2015936606

Book design by George Stevens

This publication is designed to provide accurate and authoritative information in regard to the subject matter covered. It is sold with the understanding that the publisher is not engaged in rendering legal, accounting, or other professional services. If legal advice or other expert assistance is required, the services of a competent professional person should be sought.

Advantage Media Group is proud to be a part of the Tree Neutral® program. Tree Neutral offsets the number of trees consumed in the production and printing of this book by taking proactive steps such as planting trees in direct proportion to the number of trees used to print books. To learn more about Tree Neutral, please visit **www.treeneutral.com**. To learn more about Advantage's commitment to being a responsible steward of the environment, please visit **www.advantagefamily.com/green**

Advantage Media Group is a publisher of business, self-improvement, and professional development books and online learning. We help entrepreneurs, business leaders, and professionals share their Stories, Passion, and Knowledge to help others Learn & Grow. Do you have a manuscript or book idea that you would like us to consider for publishing? Please visit **advantagefamily.com** or call **1.866.775.1696.**

To Stephen Michael Margaritis: Embrace and build on the power of improvisation, because someday your ideas will change the world. I love you!

acknowledgments

I would like to start by thanking my father and mother for everything that they sacrificed so I could grow up to achieve my dreams and goals. I especially have to thank my father for instilling humor into my life. He was a funny man. When I would bring a girlfriend home, my father would greet her by saying "Son, she is a lot better looking than you described. Here's $5, go to the store and buy yourself something while I talk to your girlfriend." Thanks Dad! I love you and miss you.

I would also like to thank the most influential person in my life, the chairman of my board, my wife Mary. Without her support, guidance, leadership, compassion, and love, I could not pursue my passion. We have been married for about 20 years, and we are always by each other's side, never in front or behind—side-by-side.

A very special thanks go to my brother and sister Steve and Stacie, for being the best brother and sister a guy could ever have—I love you both!

A special thanks go to George Caleodis, who introduced me to the art of improvisation; Joan McGloshen, who helped me get started in the speaking business; Dr. Gary Previts, without his support, I would have never become a CPA; J. Clarke Price, who has been a great mentor and friend; Bob Sheasley who helped make writing this book a lot of fun, along with Advantage Media Group!

There are so many family and friends that I want to thank but I can't begin to list you all because there would be no room for the content of the book. So a warm and loving THANK YOU to you all (y'all for my Kentucky family and friends.)

Go CATS!

foreword

Overcoming shyness or meeting the challenge of having meaningful engagements with strangers—or even meaningful conversations with coworkers—plagues too many of us in the workforce. Why is that? What is it about really listening and reacting that is so difficult for so many of us?

This book uses the simple act of improvisation to help you develop new skills and new approaches that will improve your ability to react to and interact with others.

When you hear the word "improvisation", you may immediately think, "I'm not funny; this won't work for me." However, the tips that follow will help you overcome natural reluctance and self-consciousness and will show you how to have richer conversations and build more robust relationships.

Improvisation isn't about being funny. It's not about being quick to react and getting a laugh. Through this book, you'll learn basic tips and skills that will help you listen to those around you, learn how to react to what they're saying, and have better, more meaningful conversations.

Improv is No Joke is a quick read packed with practical tips and examples of how to apply the simple principles of improvisation. The author's passion for the world of stand-up comedy and improvisation—and his personal experience in applying that passion to the business world—provides tips that everyone can apply in their everyday life.

The simple art of paying attention to the people with whom you're talking and really listening to what they're saying happens all too infrequently. It's up to every one of us to improve the day-to-day interactions we have with coworkers, clients, and customers. This book will help you become a more effective listener and more effective at having the sort of meaningful conversations that can lead to long-term relationships.

J. Clarke Price, FASAE, CAE

contents

Beyond the Spreadsheet

"I just want to thank you," said a woman who approached me after I had concluded my third presentation at a two-day seminar for CPAs in Tennessee. "This has meant a lot to me."

And then tears began to well up in her eyes. "Are you okay?" I asked her.

"Pete, I'm on the verge of getting a divorce," she said, "and we are at the 11th hour—but now I'm thinking we need to hold off.

"In fact," she said through her sobs, "I'm going home tonight to see if I can save my marriage."

She told me that she realized that she had been controlling and hadn't truly been listening to her husband. She had come to understand that her personality type—headstrong and dominant—works in some ways but wasn't exactly resulting in wedded bliss. She told me that she realized the problem wasn't him. It was her.

She sniffled and wiped at her eyes. I hope I had the presence of mind to hand her a tissue—I wasn't all that accustomed to dealing with crying accountants.

My final talk that day had been "Embrace your inner superhero." As in many of my presentations, I emphasized the principles of improvisation, which include supporting, respecting, trusting, listening, focusing, and adapting.

I had pointed out that true leadership involves the ability to drop your own agenda and truly focus on others and listen to understand them, not just wait until you get your opening to respond. It's one of the "soft skills" that accountants and other left-brained, logical, and linear thinkers must master if they wish to advance beyond the numbers to attain greater success.

I had told the audience about my own revelation on the importance of listening. We all have expectations for our children. Some might be happy if the kids just stay out of jail, but most people want them to grow up to make important contributions to our world.

When my son, Stephen, was in second and third grade, I tried to help him as often as possible with his homework assignments. I was a college accounting professor at Ohio Dominican University at the time, so I had more flexibility with after-school availability than did my wife, whose position as general manager of a Macy's department store was highly demanding.

Every day, I battled with Stephen to get him to do his homework. I felt frustrated, because I was intent on helping him avoid the same mistakes that I had made. Our conversations would go like this:

"Stephen, I need you to read this chapter."

"Dad, I don't like to read."

"Well, Stephen, if you don't read, there's going to be no TV tonight."

"Dad, I really hate to read."

I would switch gears. "Okay, Stephen, let's try your math."

"Dad, I just don't like math. I don't like those story problems."

"Sure you do, Stephen, you do those in class. Come on, let's do your homework."

"I really don't want to do math right now, Dad. I really don't understand it. Can I just go play basketball?"

"Stephen, finish your homework or there's no TV and no Xbox for the rest of the week."

This got to be so bad that every day I felt I had to put my armor on, because I knew that he and I were going to go to battle after school. Homework time became fight time.

This went on for months, until we mentioned the problem to the pediatrician. "You might want to talk to somebody about this," she said. "There might be something else there."

We made an appointment to have him see a psychologist for tests. I'll never forget the moment when we got the results: "Mr.

and Mrs. Margaritis, your son has a moderately severe case of ADHD along with a reading disorder."

I was speechless. I was thinking, "Oh my God, *what?* ADHD this whole time? I've been so overbearing and short with him. I haven't been listening to him." Stephen had been giving me clues along the way, and I didn't recognize them. I felt that I'd messed up, that I hadn't been caring, that I'd been controlling.

It was like a punch in the gut. I felt like a dreadful parent. Stephen hadn't known how to communicate to me that there was something wrong. He wanted to tell me this: "Dad, I can't seem to focus, I can't pay attention for long, and when I read stuff, I don't understand it." I had just thought he was being lazy and willful and that *he* was trying to control *me*.

We gave a lot of consideration to the best way to help him and decided medication would be appropriate in his case. Overnight it seemed, Stephen went from being this kid who fought me tooth and nail over his homework to a kid who was excited about it. His grades got better, and his self-esteem improved dramatically. He became an eager and curious student.

Seeing Stephen's transformation, my wife and I wished we had taken action a few years earlier to help him get a better head start. But we hadn't truly listened. We had an agenda, and that agenda had clouded our ability to hear what our son was trying to tell us. We all changed. We began to listen in a more meaningful way.

That was the lesson on listening that apparently had touched the heart of that tearful woman who approached me at the conference.

Often, after I have delivered that talk, people have come up to me with comments such as "I applaud you for doing what you did and realizing that you weren't listening—because my brother [or sister or cousin] went through something very much like that." They share stories about how parents so often have their own agenda and become controlling to the point where they no longer can truly hear their kids. It's frustrating for children when they need to communicate something and don't know how to begin and just seem to get in trouble if they try.

When the psychologist gave us the diagnosis, I asked: "Are you talking about Stephen or me?" I explained that I'd had my own journey with ADHD and that maybe Stephen had inherited some of my traits. I just hope he develops a sense of humor about himself.

What I learned was that this was a case of the parent needing to listen, not of the child needing to listen. Parents tend to have a vision for their children and become determined that they fit that mold. They simply tell the kids what they must do—and that can lead to a variety of problems.

A fundamental of improvisation that I advocate whenever I speak to audiences is the principle of "yes, and..." As I will explain in this book, those two words have changed my life. It's an approach that opens possibilities, as opposed to the stifling effect of "yes, but...," the words that we so often use instead.

Several minutes after I spoke to that woman after my presentation, another audience member approached me. He was a retired CPA and a former marine.

"Pete, that was the best thing I've heard in a long time. I really hope that you will be coming back here again." He sent me an email the next day: "Keep it up. You're making a difference in people's lives."

People often approach me with words of appreciation. Whenever I can, I try to meet people and learn about them and learn from them. You have to keep moving forward. I look at every opportunity as a "yes, and…" moment for growth and development.

As an accountant, I know that there is a time to get up and get away from the numbers. You have to lift your nose from the books and see the expressions on people's faces. You will see things there that you will never see on paper.

Or, as one of my clients once told a detail-oriented associate: "You know, sometimes you just have to step away from the effing spreadsheet, and now is the time."

chapter 1

Entrée into Improv

I can still see my son as a newborn, lying in the car seat as we brought him home from the hospital. I was driving ever so slowly and carefully.

I looked over at my wife. "They didn't give us a manual," I said.

Fourteen years later, as I speak to audiences, I often ask: "How many of you have kids?" A lot of hands go up. "Well, then," I say, "you certainly know from experience what it means to improvise."

A lot of people think that everything in improvisation is made up and that the points don't matter, because of the *TV Show Whose Line is it Anyway?* I don't subscribe to that thought, because everything is not made up, and the points do matter.

If you had a script for how your day would go, I'm willing to bet you would be revising it by the time you left the house. By the end of the day, your script might bear little resemblance to what you had originally intended. So much changes so fast, and life is all about reacting, adapting, and improving.

The principles of improvisation, as I've been exposed to it, are respect, trust, support, listening, focus, and adaptability. And the glue that holds those together, as we will see, is the principle of "yes, and..." The message that I emphasize in my speaking engagements is that you can find greater success in your career and in your personal life if you embrace and adapt the principles of improvisation.

I call myself "The Accidental Accountant™." I am a person who has a whole brain, meaning my right brain and my left brain are equally dominant, with a message that could help people in many walks of life—and in that sense, maybe I'm not such an accident after all.

When we think about left-brain people, we think about stereotypical accountants: They are seen as brainy with critical and analytical skills and an ability to work independently, but they are also seen as introverted and kind of nerdy and socially awkward. I love watching the TV show *The Big Bang Theory*. I have known people in the accounting profession who are somewhat like Sheldon Cooper, lacking in social filters. I have spent 20-odd years in their world.

me out if I did that, and they did. Who comes up with such rules? In some states, it's okay to ride a motorcycle without a helmet, but you'll get a ticket if you don't wear your seat belt. I can't make connections like that…I guess I just don't fit in.

When I found comedy, I think it was a coping mechanism—although I'm pretty well grounded, unlike a lot of comics. Like Robin Williams, I found great joy in making people laugh. If I get on a roll and people start laughing, I won't stop. I'll just keep going until someone makes me stop. For some reason, though, I didn't find it overly appealing to spend my time in a bar late at night trying to make drunks laugh.

Today my hope is to get people to laugh and to think at the same time. Mel Helitzer, who was a journalism professor at Ohio University, once said: "It's not what's taught at a university but what's caught. And if we can get students' mouths open for laughter, we can slip in a little food for thought."

My teaching philosophy is similar: in order to educate, you have to entertain if you want retention and if you want outcomes. I think of myself as CEO of my own company—the Chief "Edutainment" Officer.

Nobody remembers the talking heads who just spew stuff out in a monotone. We remember what makes us laugh and when people tell us stories. We remember the pictures in our head. But we don't remember somebody just spouting a bunch of words.

I realized I could take my business knowledge and marry it to a love of comedy and a love of learning. I wanted to draw upon the skills and techniques for stand-up comedy, along with the completely different principles of improvisational comedy, and blend them to see what happened. I'd much rather talk to people about things that affect their lives than give some highly technical presentation. I've done my share of those, too.

In the coming chapters, you will see the ways that I have embraced improvisation in my business, personal, and professional life. I have learned to trust myself in a lot of different positions, in business and in life, and I feel as if I have a pretty good batting average. I've struck out sometimes, and a few times I've been hit by the pitcher. But I've recovered just fine.

My father meant the world to me, but the man did not like mistakes. If I spilled my milk, I might as well just call it a night. I remember the time he went berserk when he caught my brother making Jiffy Pop instead of regular popcorn. Such an indulgence was a mistake.

You find out only later in life that if you don't make mistakes, you're never going to grow. If you don't take risks, you're never going to grow. Accepting failure is part of learning. The idea is to try not to repeat those mistakes—a very simple concept lost in the corporate world, where blame is the "Yes, but..."

A major lesson that I got from improv is that it's okay to make mistakes, learn from them, and just keep moving forward. I have used improvisation in various aspects of my life to tackle business challenges, to deal with health issues, and to learn to be a better father and husband.

Cocktails out Their Noses

When I worked at Victoria's Secret, my colleagues knew I did stand-up comedy and improv, so they asked me once to be the opening act for an evening of entertainment at a leadership retreat. The company had booked a sketch comedy troupe from Columbus called Shadowbox.

I was eager to comply—it would be fun to bring some humor to the daily doings of the business. The company president, the CFO, and a lot of vice presidents and senior managers—basically, people who could fire me—would be there.

Two days before the show, I felt nervous. What was I doing? In comedy, it's a thin line between being a hero and being a bomb. If I bombed, how would the bosses view me? I wondered if I might lose my job.

And then I realized this was a classic case of my listening to the "inner critic"—that infernal internal voice within each of us, the one that natters and annoys and tries to convince us of our failings. I needed a heathy dose of improv for my attitude. I was telling myself a whole slew of "what ifs"—all of them negative.

One of the themes that I have emphasized is courage, which, in my mind, is another way of saying the capacity to accept risk. We need to face our fears. So I thought: "How about this for a change? I will picture myself knocking it out of the park and the next day at work they're carrying me up and down the halls and calling me the funniest thing since *Seinfeld*."

As it turned out, I performed for ten minutes to an appreciative crowd. We're talking belly laughs. We're talking cocktails spewing out of noses. I was taking shots at the president of the company and at the CFO, and it was working. That night, one of the senior managers called me to say, "Pete, I think I just witnessed a major piece of courage. You put yourself out there in front of people who could fire you in a second, and you just slayed them all."

That night, I believe, was my buy-in. That's when I realized, "This stuff actually does work." I had gone into the lion's den and come out unscratched. I had employed the principles of both stand-up and improvisation. I had written funny lines but not offensive ones, and I'd been prepared enough to make it all work. The principles of improv had all come together. The risk had yielded the reward.

There's risk in everything we do, and improvisation involves the ability to take risks while understanding that some things won't work out. You have to accept the fact that you will fail—but through failure, you grow. If we just take the easy path, we miss out on life. We don't put ourselves out there to explore what we can do.

I'm cautious about life-threatening risks, of course, but one must consider the ramifications of all risks. I've become much stronger in my ability to assess them. Being an accountant is challenging, especially when you have ADHD and a bit of dyslexia. It's like hiring Robin Williams to do your taxes—"good mooorning, IRS!"

And yet I can say that I have never had so much fun since I took the risk of starting my own business. At first, I just wanted to talk about the soft skill topics. Then the economy fell apart, and I moved toward the technical side, since accountants still needed to get their continuing education. I adapted to the situation and shifted my business model—but as soon as we came out of that recession I moved back toward my true passion.

So Who Is This Guy?

So just who is this Peter Margaritis, anyway? When I pronounce my last name, it sounds like a drink special in a Key West bar owned by Jimmy Buffett. I much prefer that to the pronunciation I often hear that rhymes with hepatitis, gingivitis, and laryngitis—I don't want people thinking they need to take a Z-Pak to hang out with me.

At the airport recently in Columbus, the TSA agent commented about my name: "Well! I bet it's always five o'clock at *your* house!" As I moved onward in the line, I heard her explaining to the next person: "Yeah, can you believe it, his name's Margaritis—like the drink, you know? *Margaritas!*"

In fact, when I check into a hotel, about 90 percent of the time I'll hear a quick quip like "Hey, hey, I bet you're quite the partier!" The clerk will smile while waiting for me to join in his insight, and then speak more slowly: "Margaritis. Wow. Wish I were you."

"That's the first time I've ever heard that," I respond, and we both laugh. Sarcasm at its best.

I know a lot of the technical side of accounting, not taxes, in all its excruciating detail, and all the left-brain stuff. But my passion is the right-brain stuff, those soft skills—and that's what I bring to audiences in my speaking engagements.

You can get tips on the balance sheet and tax advice in a million places, but don't expect that in this book. Instead, I will talk about what people truly need to know first. In my speaking gigs, I discuss things such as leadership and creativity, communication and networking, public speaking, and professional etiquette. Those might not be qualities that come first to mind when describing the stereotypical CPA. But remember, I am The Accidental Accountant™—and I know those qualities are essential for anyone who hopes to build a clientele.

I have never been a CEO or a CFO, and I don't run a firm, but I have chaired the executive board of the Ohio Society of CPAs—and I'm hardly the typical person in that role. People wonder how I got to such positions and where my skill set came from. Well, I do have my master's in accountancy, and I do have my experience at Price Waterhouse and Victoria's Secret. I have also been an accounting professor. But to a large extent, my skills grew out of my life experiences, as I have adapted to many challenges that have played major roles in preparing me for what I do today.

The Improvisation Way of Life

When people hear about "improvisation," they often think of Drew Carey and company on the TV show *Whose Line Is It Anyway?* or of the Second City troupes. But most can easily see how they do improv themselves, every single day. To improvise simply means, as the dictionary tells us, "to compose and perform on the spur of the moment and without any preparation." My definition of improvisation is that everything is not made up and the points do matter. Good improvisers must draw upon their wealth of knowledge to adapt to a variety of situations. Without that knowledge, they have nothing. It's the same in the business world. You have to have knowledge and experiences in order to improv your way to success.

At a recent presentation, my audience included people from Germany and from Brazil. A Brazilian came up to me during a break and said, "You've presented improvisation in a positive way, but in my country it is deemed to be negative." I was having a hard time with his accent, but he seemed to be telling me that in his culture, work was a humorless duty. "You showed me that it's okay," he said. "Improvisation is not about jokes, not about slapstick and hilarity."

That's right. It's a way of life. Sure, it's good for comedy. Improvisation can generate a million jokes—and that's a cool by-product of the process. But it goes far beyond comedy, and my hope is that the readers of this book will recognize ways to apply improv in their lives.

Improvisation is going with the flow. The day never goes quite as expected. The phone rings, or there's a knock at the door, and you rearrange your plans. You make decisions on the spur of the moment. Yes, it requires a change in schedule—and that's hard for a lot of people. It causes them friction and stress, and communications break down.

If you accept the fact that change is going to happen, you can adapt and adjust. You can take the "yes, and…" attitude of opportunity or the "yes, but…" attitude of defeat. You could say: "Yes, but why is this happening to poor me?" or "Yes, but I don't have time for this." Or you could say: "Yes, and now I get to do this!" In other words, "yes, and…" is positive in nature. It's not a downer. It's a way of celebrating the possibilities in life without letting the doubts crush you.

Some people—and accountants in particular—are very linear in their thinking and don't like surprises. They don't want anything to disrupt their day. But they have to accept it. They can choose their attitude, positive or negative—but let me assure you, you will go further with a positive attitude.

A speaker named Nobby Lewandowski once told me that attitude is an acronym for "all the time, integrity, tenacity, understanding, determination, and enthusiasm." It's a far more pleasant way of life.

Listening with a Group Mind

Improvisation is about teaching your mind to explore different directions rather than getting stuck on one track. That's a concept from the book *Improv Yourself: Business Spontaneity at the Speed of Thought*, by Joseph A. Keefe.

We need to listen to truly understand instead of listening to respond. To have a truly engaging conversation, you have to park your agenda. When you can do that, you can truly listen and respond to what the other person is saying. The conversation grows much richer. You are focusing on the other person instead of thinking about what you want to say next.

Let's say a CPA has a client across the table who is pouring out his angst about what's keeping him up at night. The client is making it clear what he needs and wants, but the CPA is thinking of which services he might provide and is waiting for his opening.

"Well," he tells the long-faced client, "we have this new product here that we've developed..."

The client wonders whether the CPA was listening to him—and he wasn't. He was waiting to deliver a sales pitch. Far better if he could have put those products and services to the side and truly heard his client's wants and needs and asked questions to learn more about them. A real conversation results in a meeting of minds. That's the way to a genuine sale—one that's a real fit.

Improvisation actors understand the concept of "group mind." That's when they develop a relationship with the other actors on stage, with whom they have performed before, perhaps for years. They know what the others are going to do. They know how they're going to react. It still involves close listening skills, but the actors can adapt more quickly.

Sports teams can develop that kind of ability to think in concert. So can couples. I've been married for 19 years, and we have been together for 21 years. There are times when we can have conversations with our eyes. That is a high level of improvisation. Whether on a team or in a marriage, that's the kind of group mind that works wonders.

Back into the Fire—and Out

In 2005, I was a professor at Ohio Dominican University and was helping to place students in various jobs. They were getting paid a lot more than I was, but at least I had summers off. One day I said to myself, "I want to get back into the game. I want to go back into public accounting." I resigned from the university at the end of the fall term and started full time as a tax manager for a large-sized CPA firm in Columbus.

I had been teaching tax but not really at the corporate or partnership level. My role at this firm was supposed to be much more than just a tax accountant. I believed I was going to help with the education and mentoring of the younger staff. But that was not the case. This was going to be primarily a technical tax position.

I started January 2 and was thrown right into the fire. It soon became obvious that technically I was in way over my head. By early March, I was starting to see work go around me, not through me. I went into the partners' office and had one of those critical but uncomfortable conversations that accountants, in particular, really don't like to have.

"I know I'm in over my head," I said, "and I know that you're pushing work around me. We can do one of two things. We can say this was a bad experiment and I can leave now, or you can keep me on, and I can help you in some way, shape, or form get through April 15, and then we'll go our separate ways." The partners agreed to the latter path, and by June of 2006 I left the firm.

I had taken a huge risk by going back into that environment after more than ten years out of public accounting. But I don't look at it as a failure. I learned a lot about the mentality and angst today in accounting firms, which has helped me to tailor some of my programs.

It was a rich experience. I learned a lot about myself. I'm not the type of person who wants to keep track of every six minutes of the day and charge a client for it. I also understand more about how people think and operate in a CPA office and what the partners, managers, and staff are facing. I've been able to take all that away and build it into my programming.

Those insights were a victory for me. Communication skills have become increasingly critical in the accounting profession, even more than analytical skills. CPA firms have been doing things the same way for a long time. They say they've changed, but actually they haven't. If I were building a firm today, I would make sure I had technical people, of course, but I would want more people with the ability to communicate, interact, network, sell, and present.

When first-year staff members come on board at a CPA firm, they're inundated. Stuff is coming at them at 100 miles an hour. Nobody is teaching them. I have developed a curriculum that I call "Backpack to briefcase: A transition from college senior to first-year staff," based on an idea from a good friend, Paul Weisinger. The course addresses things that nobody talks about but that everyone needs to know, such as professional etiquette. That doesn't mean where to put the knife and the fork. It's about communicating within an organization. It's about dealing with policies. It's about dressing properly, the risks of office romance, and using cell phones and sending emails.

Getting an education requires more than passing an exam. You need to meet people. Networking these days is not just about LinkedIn. You still have to go face to face and toe to toe with others. That's the only way you can get a gut feeling—the only way you will know whether to back away or draw nearer. You don't get that feeling online. You need to be eyeball to eyeball to develop a sense of professional skepticism.

I'd seen many new hires come in. They'd be shown the accounting software and the files and how to conduct an audit or compile a tax return. It became clear to me that they weren't getting some of those critical communication skills—and I knew that my curriculum was moving in the right direction.

That direction has been harder to maintain in recessionary times. It's hard enough to get CPAs and accountants to recognize a return on investment for soft skills courses. But I counter with this: What's the return on investment if your people can't communicate? If they need an acronym to understand, then I ask what is the RONI—risk of not investing. Sometimes I hear the argument that people are going to leave anyway, so why pay for anything but technical training? That was the thinking of decades past—and it means that your next round of hires will be leaving you, too, because you aren't willing to invest in their overall career.

In the book *The Second Machine Age*, authors Brynjolfsson and McAfee discuss how computing power doubles every 18 to 24 months (Moore's law) and the implications thereof. In 2015, there are cars that drive themselves and 3-D printers that can crown a tooth in two hours instead of two weeks. The authors state that repetitive jobs will be replaced by machines. Just look what Amazon did in automating the shipping process through robotics, which helped increase efficiency in their warehouses in 2014. The accounting profession has a lot of repetitive processes. The authors state that the way to beat the machine is through communication, collaboration, and creativity.

My goal, in the accounting profession, is to change the conversation to recognize that communication skills are in a lot of ways much more important to society than solid analytics. If you can't communicate without using accountant-speak, your client may never know what you are talking about. You will sound to them like Charlie Brown's teacher—"waa waa wo waa waa…"

That's what I really learned from that foray back into public accounting. I worked hard every day, but it didn't work out. Afterward, I wished I could have stayed and done something else there. Had I succeeded, however, I probably would be beating my head against a wall—and I would not be doing what I do today. Through that setback, I discovered a new path, on which I can emphasize the lessons and skills that matter most if accountants want to do well with their clients.

Life's a journey. Some of the steps we take might not make sense until later, when we see the reason. I truly believe that many of my life experiences—my restaurant and banking and professorial days, for example—were meant to set me up for what I'm doing today. There was a reason I was doing that stuff.

I wouldn't trade any of it. I am living my passion. We all have different dreams. If someone's dream is to make managing partner in an accounting firm, I say go for it. Do whatever it takes to get there. Start your own firm if you must. Figure out the risks, and do what is necessary to get the reward.

"I don't think I've ever seen you this happy before," my wife has been telling me for several years now. That wasn't what she saw when I was playing the corporate game. That just wasn't me.

Rolling with the Changes

My life changed the day I recognized the principles of improv and "yes, and…" and began applying them day in and day out. It hasn't happened overnight, but it has really allowed me to do what I want to do.

I have found that there are a lot of prima donnas in the speaking business. Some people can be tough to work with. I try to stay low-key, and it's a quality that others appreciate. I can lose my cool, but I try very hard to maintain control. I try to adapt to any situation.

I flew into Los Angeles recently for three days of webcasts in Glendale—and on my way there I got an email saying I was actually supposed to have been sent to Irvine, an hour away in the other direction. I just went to the hotel in Glendale and waited until those involved figured it out, and it worked out fine.

"You were so low-key about it," my client told me later. "You just adapt to almost any situation."

That's what I try to do. I could have thrown a hissy fit about that scheduling snafu, but I'd rather "roll with the changes," as REO Speedwagon put it. We need to learn to adapt.

I've been rolling with unexpected turns my whole career. I've been a restaurant manager. I was a headhunter for a time. I repossessed cars. I was a banker. I was an accountant for a big four accounting firm. I worked for Victoria's Secret Catalogue—I used to tell people I worked in women's underwear every day. I was a university professor. I've adjusted to changes inside and outside the profession of accounting, and today I've found my niche. I'm an entrepreneur.

In the chapters ahead, we'll take a closer look at some of those soft skills that are my passion. We'll examine the nature of improvisation—and what it is not.

Here's what it is not: Improvisation is not making stuff up out of thin air, and it's far more than just a way to come up with a million jokes—although good improvisers are funny. It's not about disorder and stalling. Those are the negative connotations that the gentleman from Brazil must have had in mind.

Rather, improvisation is about assessing the needs of a situation by listening, understanding, adapting, and taking action to address issues as they arise. To be good at improv, you need to understand your strengths and weaknesses and be able to operate in confusing situations. By listening and focusing, you can cut through that chaos and find clarity. And you have to be willing to take risks. You need to avail yourself of opportunities and avoid excuses as to why you think things won't work out.

Improvisation is the ability to think on your feet, adapt to any situation, and make your teammates look good. You might not think of yourself as part of a team, but if you work for an organization, that's a team. If you're in a department, that's a team. In other words, it's not just about you, and that is particularly true for leaders.

I think back again to the day we brought Stephen home from the hospital. My wife had read a lot of books about raising a child, but we still had to think on our feet in the throes of projectile vomiting and toxic diapers. We adapted to a colicky child. We had to trust, support, respect, focus, listen, adapt, and use the power of "yes, and…" every single day.

Chapter 1 Takeaways

⇨ The principles of improvisation are supporting, trusting, respecting, focusing, listening, and adapting.

⇨ The glue to improvisation are these two powerful words of "yes, and...," which inspire, motivate, and help keep things moving in the right direction.

⇨ "Yes, and..." is about agreement, not about always agreeing.

How can you begin to incorporate the principles of improvisation into your daily life?

chapter 2

"Yes, and..."

"Hi, my name is Becky, and I'm a stand-up comedian. I've performed at Joker's Comedy Club," said one of my classmates as we introduced ourselves at the improvisation workshop.

"Hi, my name is Craig," said another, "and I'm an actor. I've been in some off-Broadway plays."

And then it was my turn. "Hi, my name is Pete. I'm a CPA."

"Oh yeah?" someone said. "So what show did you play that on?"

"No, I didn't play it on a show," I explained. "I really am a CPA."

Everyone tilted their heads in a Scooby-Doo type moment: "Erruh?" I know they were all thinking, "Heh, heh—*nerd!*" I was just hoping they might like me for something other than free tax advice. This was my first experience with improv, and I wanted to fit in.

Each of us was asked to participate in a scene. My first partner was Craig, who pretended he was casting a fishing line. "What a great day to go fishing!" he told me.

"Craig, we're not fishing. We're riding a horse at the Kentucky Derby." I thought that was clever.

"Hold on, stop, stop," the instructor said and addressed me: "What you just did, CPA man, was you negated his reality."

"Negated his what, dude?"

"Yeah, Craig told us that he was doing something and you said no, he wasn't. You negated his reality. Now, you and Craig do that scene again."

I didn't recall saying no, but I was game for another shot at it.

"What a great day to be fishing!" Craig exclaimed.

"Craig, we're sitting by the pool, bathing in some rays."

"Stop!" the teacher shouted. "Pete, take a break, okay? Sit down and watch everybody, and next week we'll let you try again."

On the sidelines, I sat watching and thinking. "I can do this," I told myself. "I know I can." I told myself I would do something that those loosey-goosey left-wing normal actors would never think about doing. Should I boycott Bill Maher? Not a bad idea, but no, not that.

Instead, I was going to master this by researching improvisational comedy and learning everything I could about it. I was going to read up on Steve Carrell, Tina Fey, and John Belushi and put all the data into an Excel spreadsheet. I would create tables, sprinkle in a couple of VLOOKUPs, and then find the standard deviation of their individual functions. This accountant was going to see exactly what added up to success at improvisational comedy.

So I showed up the next time thinking, "I got my data, I've memorized the routines." I had figured out that they had ten laughs per minute. So I divided that by 60 to come up with a 0.1667 laughs per second. Then I consolidated it, put it on a spreadsheet, and committed it to memory. This was just like studying for the CPA exam. I was going to blow them away.

My turn came to do a scene with Becky. She was bending over slightly, both hands going in a circular motion.

"It's going to take me all day to wax this car," she said.

I thought of all those Belushi sketches I'd watched and all that I'd crammed into my head in the past week.

"Waxing a car, really?" I said. "We're short-order cooks at the Olympian Restaurant in Chicago. Cheeseburger, cheeseburger, cheeseburger! No fries or chips. No Coke or Pepsi. Or wait! We're the Killer Bees of Saturday Night!"

"Stop!" the teacher ordered. "You are negating again, and you are not listening."

"I am not negating," I protested.

"Try it again, Peter. But this time come into the scene without an agenda, without pushing your ideas onto someone else. Just use what the other person gives you, nothing else. Trust, Peter, trust."

"Okay," I thought, "I'll do it his way, and he'll see how unfunny that is. I have the data, I've done the research."

Becky bent and again made circles with her hands. "It's going to take me all day to wax this car," she said.

"Yes, and let me grab a towel and help you finish before it rains," I said.

She said, "Let's have some fun and get into a rhythm like in *The Karate Kid.*"

"Wax on!" I said. "Wax off," said she. Wax on, wax off, wax on, wax off. We joined in the rhythm—and I saw that it wasn't me who was getting laughs. *We* were getting laughs, working as a team.

The teacher was standing offstage, clapping, as was the rest of the class. And then I got it. I absolutely got it. The key to connecting with another person was to drop my agenda and listen. Success was not about *me*. Success was about *us*.

Listening to Understand

I often ask audiences this question: "Do you listen to respond, or do you listen to understand?" Then I pause, and the looks I see on people's faces seem to say, "Oh, there's a difference?"

When someone is talking, how often are people not really listening but rather just waiting for their chance to say what they know? "Hurry up and finish," they are thinking, "because I'm the one with something profound to say."

That's listening to respond versus listening to understand. The latter requires you to put your agenda to the side, listen to what the other person is saying, and pause to gather your thoughts or let the other person reflect. Then you can ask a question or perhaps say something more pertinent to the conversation.

Good salespeople do this all the time. They listen to the wants and needs expressed by their potential customer or client, they ask some questions to better understand those desires, and then they adapt a response to meet them. But many salespeople just know their pitch. They have a new product or service and can't wait to talk about all the advantages and features—and their prospects end up looking elsewhere for someone who will listen to them.

We've all been there. One salesperson begins blathering away, and we glaze over. Another actually engages us, gets us to think twice, and scores—because that one actually seems to care about the other human being in the conversation. The customer feels a sense of trust, which tends to lead to a purchase. Nobody is eager to buy from someone spewing forth some well-practiced patter. We tune out people like that.

I once was pitching a proposal for a creativity course to a man I'd known a long time, a managing partner in his firm. We had been talking about this for many months, and he liked the course plan that I had written. "I like what you're doing, Pete," he said, "and how it's laid out, but I'm just a little nervous stepping over that cliff and going down this path with my partners."

"Well, tell you what, I'm doing this course with a firm in New Jersey next week," I told him. "I'll give you my contact person's information, and after I do this course I'll send you the evaluations, too. See what you think, and then we'll talk."

"Pete, I told you I liked the course," he said, surprised. "I was expecting you to say, 'I'll send you a proposal tomorrow.'"

"But that's not what I heard you say," I explained. "You said you were nervous about bringing this to your partners. I heard everything you were telling me, not just the part I wanted to hear." I heard exactly what he was saying, even when he wasn't hearing himself. That's what it means to listen to understand. When you are hearing more than your own words, you pick up on people's signals.

Listening well and communicating effectively are critical skills in every aspect of our lives, both personal and business. Such moments opened my eyes to deeper relationships. I have learned to listen better and to appreciate others. I'd been applying some of those skills instinctively, but there was so much more to grasp. It took a while for it to sink in, and it takes a while to change.

Mr. Know-It-All

A common game used to develop improvisational listening skills is called "Mr. Know-It-All." It helps people to drop their agenda, listen, and focus—to be in the moment.

In the game, I ask for three volunteers and put them in three chairs facing the audience. "Together, these people are Mr. Know-It-All," I say, "and can answer any question—but just one word at time." To demonstrate, I ask: "Why is the sky blue?" I tap the first person's shoulder, then the next, and the next, and each provides a word as they attempt to construct a sentence to answer my question.

"The...sky...is...blue...because...," they begin, and by then each volunteer is invariably forming an agenda for how they think the statement should proceed. When a player says a word that doesn't fit that agenda, the others get flustered and have to scramble for a response.

As a result, the sentence tends to ramble in ridiculous directions. "So what happened here?" I ask, and someone usually explains it this way: "Well, I had an idea in mind, but this guy next to me said a different word, and it threw me down a different path, and I didn't know what to do."

"Let's try it again," I say, "and this time don't have anything in your head. Just listen to what the other person says, and then build off of it to make the sentence as accurate—and maybe as funny—as it can be." It takes a couple times, but it works. They begin to listen to understand, not just to respond. They drop their agendas. They stop trying to control how they want this thing to go.

It's interesting to see them have that "aha!" moment. When I do this exercise at speaking engagements, I usually ask the first two questions and then solicit one from the audience. "Anyone have a question for Mr. Know-It-All?" I ask. Once, a woman stood up in the back of the room and called out, "Why do men cheat?" The three volunteers began like this: "Because…we… can…," at which point I quickly announced, "Game over!" Mr. Know-It-All doesn't need to become Dr. Phil.

The Eyes Can Listen

We need to learn to listen with our eyes as well as our ears. Perhaps you have had this happen to you at a networking event: Someone introduces himself and asks a question, and as soon as you start to answer you can see that his eyes are scoping out the next victim.

He might be nodding, but you don't feel any real eye contact; it's as if he's looking through you. The eyes are the windows to the soul, and they reveal so much—including a lack of interest.

In improv, you learn about listening with the eyes. You have to carefully observe your surroundings. Unless you understand your scene, how can you adapt and respond appropriately?

You need to listen with your ears, to understand, and also listen to your physical environment. By listening with your eyes, you can gain the greater context. What is the body language that other people use? Are they engaged, or are their eyes glazing over? You need to know so that you can adapt and not lose them for good.

Listening with your eyes can include looking for details that can become points of connection. For example, when I meet with someone in their office, I do a quick inventory of the decor to find points on which to bond. "I see you're a Reds fan," for example, or "The Browns have luck on their side—bad luck." Or, "I see you have three daughters." I just look for some little thing to help me make a quick connection and learn a little bit more.

Two Words That Changed My Life

The two words that truly changed my life are "yes, and…" As you read the stories in this book, you no doubt are seeing that those two words in some way play a role in all of them. They are words that keep conversations going. They inspire people and spur creativity. They help to overcome resistance and fears and lead to a meeting of minds, and as such they are valuable words to use during negotiations.

We live in a "yes, but..." society. In a restaurant, you might hear the wait staff saying, "Yes, but this is not my section," or "Yes, but I'm getting ready to go on break." Those two words are far from inspiring. In fact, they deflate, and they kill creativity.

I often play the "yes, and..." game with audiences. It goes something like this: The first participant announces, "Yes, I'm a walrus." The next person might say, "Yes, you're a walrus, and you've got some really big whiskers." And another person says, "Yes, you do have really big whiskers, and you've got a big tusk." And we go down that path. Or another scenario: "Yes, I love to play golf on Saturdays." The next person says, "Oh, I love to play golf on Saturdays. And then I love to come home and sit on the patio." "Oh, yes, I love sitting on the patio and petting my chocolate lab." "Oh, yes, I love picking the fleas out of her fur and squishing them."

And so while playing this game, each participant starts off finding a level of agreement with what the preceding person said, then steers the story down a completely different path through improvisation. It always elicits a lot of laughs.

The concept of "yes, and..." is about being agreeable. It's not about agreeing, but it's about continuing the conversation. That concept is central to *Whose Line Is It Anyway?* The actors find a point of agreement and then move onward from there.

Yes, you can try that at home, kids. Or at work. If a colleague suggests an idea, you might say, "Yes, and we could explore that idea and see if we could get it in the budget next year," rather than "Yes, but there's just no money to do that." Even if you don't ultimately agree on a way to make the idea fly, you at least have been agreeable, and thereby you have shown respect and support for your associate. You are promoting an atmosphere of acceptance and possibilities, not one of rejection and defeat. The workplace culture thrives. It becomes one of inspiration, not deflation. People aren't thinking, "Why bother suggesting anything, because nobody wants to hear it." They are thinking, "This is a place where ideas are welcome."

Silencing the Inner Critic

Your inner critic will gnaw away at your confidence and slow you down. You might want to apply for a leadership position, for example, and the inner critic says you just don't have what it takes.

I was attending the Ohio Society of CPAs annual members summit and listening to the chair of the executive board talk about the society and the state of the profession.

I began thinking, "I want to be chair of the OSCPA—but the inner critic spoke up to try to talk me out of it. "Yes, you want to be the chair, but you don't have the credentials for the position. Yes, but you're not a managing partner, and you're not even in a firm. Yes, but you have only been in the profession for 20 years."

With my newfound confidence, I replaced "yes, but…" with "yes, and…," and some amazing things began to happen. "Yes, I want to be the chair, and I need to volunteer more and make myself more visible. Yes, and I need to chair some committees. Yes, and I need to get to know the staff and the CEO better. Yes, and…"

To make a long story very short, as a result of my attitude shift and developing a plan and a strategy, I was installed as chair of the executive board of the OSCPA in June 2010. I just found a different way to achieve that goal—and that way was through the power of "yes, and…"

I'm not a managing partner of an accounting firm. I'm not even a senior manager. I'm not a CFO. I'm not a controller of a company. I'm not an SVP in some bank. I'm just me. I'm this guy who came into the accounting profession late in life and who has a different view on management and leadership. I'm a guy who adopted and embraced the concept of "yes, and…" and who believes he can do anything as long as he remembers those two words.

And so if the voice of the inner critic is "yes, but…," then the means to silence that voice is "yes, and…" Some people try to drown out the sound of their inner critic by developing an ego that is twice as loud. Far better to insist on listening to the possibilities. Why shoot down someone's ideas? Let those flowers grow. "Yes, and…" is the fertilizer for creativity. "Yes, but…" stunts and kills it.

Yes, You Can Fly

A couple weeks after my initial experience at the improvisation class, my four-year-old son came up to me and said, "Hey, Dad, can I fly around the house in my Superman cape?"

"No! You kidding me? Who knows what you're going to break," I said. "You're going to make the dogs crazy. Just sit down and watch TV."

I watched him walk over to the television, his head bowed, his shoulders slumped—and I realized that I hadn't listened to him. I had shot down his playfulness. I started to realize, for the first time, how much I negate other people's ideas. I had been doing it with my family, my son, my in-laws, my clients, associates, bosses, peers, the dry cleaner, and the Starbucks barista.

I was trying to control everything. I realized I was trying so hard to get things to go my way that I'd been stepping over people, negating, and not valuing their contributions. And I'd been doing that for quite a while with my son. It was time for a healthy dose of "yes, and…"

"Hey, Stephen!" I called after him. "Yes, you can fly around the house in your Superman cape—yes, and I will be Lex Luthor, hiding from you!" His eyes widened, he smiled broadly, and we played Superman versus Lex Luthor for the next half hour.

Chapter 2 Takeaways

⇨ "Yes, and…" will silence your inner critic.

⇨ "Yes, and…" will help you achieve your dreams.

⇨ Listening requires the use of your ears and your eyes and parking your agenda.

Challenge—I challenge you to use "yes, and…" and eliminate "yes, but…" You can do this with your department, your team, and your family. Keep a "yes, but…" jar visible, and anytime someone uses "yes, but…" they have to put a dollar in the jar. After 21 days the contributions to the "yes, but…" jar will have slowed dramatically, and you can donate the money to charity or take your group out for a celebration.

chapter 3

It's Who You Know

I n the fall of 2008, I was teaching full time at Ohio Dominican University in Columbus and was beginning to move my speaking business from the soft skills to the more technical aspects of accounting. The soft skills were less in demand because of the recession.

I had mentioned this to Clarke Price, who was chief executive officer of the Ohio Society of CPAs, and he suggested that I attend a conference in February 2009 of the state CPE (continuing professional education) directors from the East Coast. He said that this would be a great networking venue, so I got the information and signed up for the conference.

I knew only two people in attendance—Clarke and Boyd Search, who was the vice president of education and training at the OSCPA. Clarke and Boyd introduced me around, and for two and a half days I talked with people, looking for opportunities.

One of those introductions would have a profound impact on my business. I was introduced to Pam Devine of the Business Learning Institute, the learning affiliate of the Maryland Association of CPAs. I told her that I taught technical accounting courses and specialized in international financial reporting standards (IFRS) and that I was building a course at ODU. I was focusing on the international financial reporting standards that, to date, have yet to be incorporated in the United States. (In 2012, I published an article titled "Is IFRS the New Metric System in the United States?") Pam was curious and took my card and my Twitter handle.

Around April, I got a tweet from Pam asking whether I was available in June and to give her a call. She needed an instructor to teach two eight-hour courses on IFRS. The instructor who had been scheduled for the courses had been fired, and she needed a replacement.

This was not an area that a lot of people understood, but she knew that I was involved in the course at Ohio Dominican. "You would have to develop your own materials," she said. "You would have to put your own slide show together, your own PowerPoints. You'll have to put all of that together because all of our thought leaders create their own content."

I accepted the opportunity. She asked how the course at ODU was coming along, and I assured her that all was well with it. After I hung up the phone, I turned to my wife and told her I needed to go into full lockdown mode until June. I hadn't started anything with the course at ODU.

I had to build this all from scratch within two months, and I did. That June, I delivered two days of presentations, and I was able to use my humor and technical knowledge. I got good reviews from the attendees. In fact, those reviews have resulted in the Business Learning Institute/Maryland Association of CPAs becoming my largest client. The experience has opened a lot of doors for me and really helped to launch my business. They vouched for me with the American Institute of CPAs, and I now am an AICPA instructor.

If I hadn't gone to that conference, I'm not sure where I would be now. But I took the risk, I was adaptable, and I got the gig.

All that networking started through my relationship with Clarke and Boyd and their willingness to introduce me to others. It was through networking that I had met Clarke originally. Back in 2002, when I was program chair for accounting at Franklin University, I had been talking to Steve Martin—not the wild and crazy guy but a smart and accomplished guy who had a top-notch CPA exam review course that he wanted me to introduce to my students. Steve was also the attorney for the OSCPA and knew Clarke, so I told him I'd like to meet Clarke. Steve scheduled a lunch for the three of us. Later, I learned that Clarke, wondering who I was, had called Gary Previts, who had granted me my provisional enrollment at Case Western. Gary must have said some good things—thanks, Gary.

At the conference, Clarke and Boyd vouched for me, and I know people went up to them and asked about me. I had been doing some programming for the Ohio Society, speaking at conferences and volunteering, and this was just before I became the incoming chair. It kept mushrooming from that. I try every year to attend that conference. The trip pays for itself and then some.

Power of Knowing Somebody

Networking is essential in today's business world, yet it can have a negative connotation. "You just got here because you knew somebody," people think, or they say it outright. I've heard people tell others that they got a job because they brownnosed. True, someone might have helped them open the door—but why would that in any way be wrong?

Sometimes, at a business conference, I sense that people are reluctant to introduce themselves and chat with others. Why? They perceive the other attendees as strangers—and mother always said, "Don't talk to strangers." But these don't tend to be the type of strangers she was talking about. These are people you need to meet—so how do you meet them? You stick out your hand, tell them your name, and smile. Simple as that.

This is a matter of respect. At conferences, I actually have walked away from people when they were looking over my head for their next victim and really not listening to what I was saying. They're appalled, and so I ask them: "Can you tell me the last three things that I said?" They don't know, because they weren't listening to me. If I cannot look people in the eye throughout a conversation—for example, when they approach me as I'm packing up after a presentation—I reassure them that I am still listening. Again: It's a matter of respect.

I believe that networking is one of the most important of skill sets. I try to look at every opportunity as a networking opportunity to meet somebody. Nobody gets to where they want to be on their own. Has there ever been a president, for example, who got to that height by avoiding people? I know I needed the help of others to become chair of the executive board. We all have to have pools of people we can draw on to help us. "Can you help me? Can you put me in contact with someone who can do this?" For instance, a colleague of mine named Jerry Esselstein introduced me to two of his clients who I ultimately got some work from.

It takes effort, of course. I tell people, "Take the 'net' and the 'ing' out of the word networking and what do you get? Work. That's what it is. It's not 9 to 5, but it is work nonetheless.

One Never Knows...

You never know what might happen when you meet somebody. At times we turn away from such opportunities. "I don't want to do that," we tell ourselves. "I don't want to go out there."

When I was chair of the executive board, I got a call from the Ohio Society staff asking me if I would take three speakers out to dinner who were in town to deliver a seminar the next day on international accounting and global standards.

My gut reaction was that I didn't really want to do it. "I don't know these guys," I told myself, "but I might as well, because you never know." I told my wife that the dinner was at 6:30 and I'd be home by 8:30 at the latest.

One of the speakers was a professorial type from Georgia, and another was from Connecticut. I was interested in the topics of their talks—but I didn't expect an evening of laughter and banter.

The three of us hit it off. We didn't know one another from Adam, and yet the comfort was immediate, as if we were old friends. The conversation gelled immediately. We laughed and shared stories until closing time, sometime close to midnight, when the manager told us, "Guys, it's time for you to leave. It's getting late—and besides, you don't have a high enough bar tab to be having this much fun."

I was right: You never know. One of those gentlemen became a client of mine. A nice revenue stream opened. If I had blown off that evening, I would never have met him. Cecil Nazereth had a business called IFRS Partners, and he was putting on webinars. He asked whether I would be interested in doing some webinars for his company and maybe cofacilitate in a few with him. I agreed—and that was a revenue stream for about two and a half years. Cecil introduced me to some others as well, and we cofacilitated for some large organizations, such as CCH, a Wolters Kluwer business, and on webinars.

We all reach that point in time when we ask, "Do I have to go? Do I want to go?" We hem and haw (just like the two characters in *Who Moved My Cheese*) and risk missing out. I just know that I'm glad that I went to that dinner and met those gentlemen. Not only was it a good time, but it was time well spent.

Where a Handshake Might Lead

You need to focus on relationships. You need to step out there, into new territory, and get to know people. That's what leads to friendships, which are important in themselves. And, of course, friendships often open the door to opportunities. When you shake a hand, you never know where it might lead.

Opportunities present themselves when you take the "yes, and..." approach and step out to take risks.

Some people are naturally shy, but if you use the principles of improvisation, you can get over that, and the opportunities will come flooding in. I am by nature a very shy person. When I tell this to people, they start laughing, as if to say, "Sure you are, funny man." But it's true.

I was very shy in school. My son is shy, too, and so I understand how he is feeling. I realized that I needed to get past the shyness. To this day, when I enter a room of people I don't know, I feel the shyness within me. My inner critic starts whispering, and so I tell it, "Yes, and go away!" I tell myself that I can do this. People aren't going to look at me and go screaming into the night—at least not until they get to know me.

The "yes, and..." approach gets you past the wall so that you can say hello to someone new. Again, I try to look for every opportunity to meet people. Sometimes that can be a challenge on an airplane. People tend to feel harried and tired on long trips—so if an attempt at conversation is met with a grunt, I won't push it. Otherwise, why not try? They're certainly not going to run very far on an airplane. I've experienced it both ways. I was on a flight recently from Norfolk, Virginia, to Baltimore, and my throat was tired after three days of speaking. I sat down next to a lady in her 80s. We exchanged hellos. So I listened to her stories. She just wanted to talk, and what harm was there in that? I wanted to show her respect.

We've all known it to happen: You meet somebody, and you strike a chord, and one of you says: "You know. I know somebody you might be interested in meeting." That's what breaks down shyness—if you can learn to respect and trust yourself.

Smiles Open Doors

Several years ago, I took a training course with a New York company called Mind Gym. One morning we were working on voice and movement. An actor named Craig Wroe—he has been in some episodes of *Law & Order* and was in an off-Broadway play at the time—came in to see us.

"Okay, one at a time each of us is going to leave this conference room and then walk back in and tell us a story about the first person you ever kissed romantically." The first student complied, and she began to tell her story.

"Stop, stop, stop!" Craig said. "I need you to smile."

"I am smiling," she said, but you couldn't tell from her face.

"Go back out and come in again." She did. Same thing.

Craig took her aside, and we watched as he said something to her, a short conversation. She then left the room and tried it yet again. This time her face was bright. She was smiling all over as she began her presentation. "What just happened?" the rest of us were wondering.

"When you need to smile," Craig explained to us, "I've got a surefire way that you can use to make it happen. Tell yourself, 'I love you.' Just those three words—but say it in a Southern accent. And see if you can stop yourself from smiling!"

I pass on this tip to others all the time, and I give Craig credit for it every single time. I tell people to make sure they don't say it out loud at the office, though, or somebody will get human resources involved or something.

The simple combination of networking and smiling is much more powerful than people realize. A smile attracts people to you. That opens up opportunities. It's not as if you are faking it and just glad-handing people and forcing yourself on them. People truly appreciate a smile. You will make it big in life when you naturally want to be around people with great ideas and great prospects.

It's yet one more beautiful lesson from the world of improvisation, which really is just the art of reaching out to other people and thinking in terms of our common humanity. That's what will draw people to you. They will know when you are authentic.

Do you know how you can tell whether someone is genuinely smiling? Look for the crow's feet at the outer corners of their eyes. If the smile is fake, you don't see those. I've always thought that women's wrinkles can be very attractive, particularly the ones that radiate from the eyes. That's a sign that they have smiled a lot. If the wrinkles are in the right place, why use Botox? You might want to hide the ones that indicate a lot of frowning and scowling, but be proud of those crow's feet.

Opportunities for Others

In 2003, while I was teaching accounting at Ohio Dominican University, I realized that I was working with a talented pool of students. This was when the financial community was dealing with the fallout from the Enron scandal and the new regulations of the Sarbanes-Oxley Act.

My seniors were looking for opportunities. Employment in accounting firms was increasing, although far more firms were recruiting at Ohio State University than at my school. While I was attending a seminar, I met the tax partner at Deloitte in Columbus, who gave me the name of the company's college recruiter.

I met the recruiter for lunch and brought her the resume of one of my students, Bryce Burkhardt. "You're not going to go wrong with this guy," I told her. "He is sharp." Deloitte ended up hiring him. It was the first time a big four accounting firm had hired from ODU—and one of his first jobs was to teach Deloitte associates in India. It was a huge opportunity, and, to date, he is still there and a manager.

The next year, after Deloitte saw how well he was doing, I got this call: "Pete, who else do you have for us?" The company kept asking, year after year, and hired four more of my students, until one year I answered, "Nobody."

"What do you mean you have nobody?"

"I don't have a student this time who has the aptitude or the personality to really survive the big four," I explained. "The people I've sent to you in the past are all able to adapt to the stresses and strains and the hours and the demands of your level. Right now I don't have anyone in my stall like that." I could have sent them somebody, but if that person failed, I would have lost credibility with my contacts. The networking would have been for naught.

It was all possible because I had met that tax partner, who had introduced me to the recruiter. They soon saw the qualities that my students could bring to them—and among those qualities were the soft skills that I teach, the ones that are so important for success.

One of my students that Deloitte hired was Pat, a bright senior who was a few years older than most of his classmates. He was working full time to put himself through school. His grade point average was 3.2, just under that 3.5 cut line, but he had a lot of real-life experience.

"I've got someone for you," I told the recruiter, "but you're going to have to trust me on this. He doesn't have the GPA you would want to see, but look at his work ethic. Look at what he has done. Look at the drive and determination this guy has, as well as his ability to communicate."

"Compare that with some of your traditional hires with a 3.8 who have been in a sorority or fraternity but haven't really done a whole lot outside of the program. In my mind, he's head and shoulders above the others." Pat had shown himself to be a good communicator and an eager learner who was willing to take risks—all key ingredients to success.

Such are the elements of improv: drive, determination, competitiveness, respect, and the ability to network and work with others. I was developing students who instinctively understood the value of improvisation in their lives. They might not have recognized it at the time, and frankly that wasn't how I was thinking of it as I conducted my classes. But that's exactly what I was doing.

Through networking, you can open opportunities not just for yourself but for others. You're doing a lot of good in the world that way, because those people will be influential and productive.

And that's why networking isn't inherently selfish. Sure, you can get places by knowing people—and what's bad about that? You still have to prove yourself.

You can go far in your career, in building a business—in life itself—by learning how to get along with people. We need to deal with others in ways that are not self-limiting but instead are self-expanding, through the power of improv.

I know all the "hard skills" of my profession, the left-brain technical side. I also know what will take people to the greatest heights: the right-brain people skills. And it has become my passion to help others develop those skills on the path to success.

Chapter 3 Takeaways

⇨ Treat every gathering as an opportunity to strengthen your professional network.

⇨ Successful leaders understand that in order to get things done and advance your career, you need other people to help you. You can't do it alone.

⇨ When you feel shy or unmotivated to participate in networking, let "yes, and…" help silence your inner critic so that you hurdle that brick wall.

Is there someone that you would like to meet, but you are hesitant? Challenge yourself and set a goal of meeting this person.

Power at the Podium

I have heard it suggested that a good way to get over one's fear of public speaking is to imagine that everyone in the audience is naked. I cannot say that I agree, particularly when delivering a eulogy or some other solemn intonation. I would be concerned that I might find all that skin and all those body parts out there to be somewhat distracting, even if everyone kept on their underwear.

When I ask audiences whether anyone fears public speaking, a lot of people raise a hand. I share a Seinfeld joke with them. Seinfeld said he had read that the people's number one fear is public speaking. Their number two fear is death. They would rather be in a casket than giving the eulogy. For a variety of reasons, they dread public speaking. They may feel they are not prepared, or they just might not like all the attention.

Whether you are in front of an audience or expounding upon something at a meeting, and you see all those eyeballs leveled at you, you need to employ the principles of improvisation.

One thing that does work in quelling those fears of public speaking is to silence that inner critic. The closer you get to the appointed time when you must speak, the louder and more incessant the critic becomes. You actually can get sick from the stress that the critic brings your way. You might just stay in bed, clasping a pillow to your head.

What can you do? You have to change the lines and start programming your brain to use "yes, and…" instead of "yes, but…" When you do, you develop confidence. You tell yourself, "I can do this," and the more times you repeat it, the more you will believe it.

"I did not have sex with that woman!" Bill Clinton declared, and perhaps at some point he actually believed himself, having chanted that line in his mind so often. Such programming of the brain can be used powerfully in positive ways, too. If you tell yourself "Yes, and I can do it" repeatedly as you prepare to give a talk and then deliver it, the inner critic will fade away. You will silence that droning voice of doom that cycles through all your fears: "You can't do this, you don't know what you're talking about, you're a fraud, you're going to fail, something will go wrong…"

The Perfectionist Pitfall

That last part of the inner critic's diatribe is actually very likely to come true. If you expect perfection, you are likely to be disappointed. Yes, you will make a mistake, probably more than one, and most of the time, unless it's a real blooper, the only person who knows about it is you. Your listeners won't pick up on it.

When you're overly focused on perfection, you can go into a downhill spiral if you do make some minor mistake such as forgetting to make one of your less important points. If you maintain your confidence, something like that won't trip you up. You need to accept the fact that you will make some slips. Think of them as opportunities to learn to do even better.

I have recorded a few of my presentations on video and asked people to critique me. Nine times out of ten, nobody notices my missteps. Then I ask them some specific questions: Was I pacing? Yes. Was I talking too fast? Yes. I had to point out my own flaws to them. But other times, people have noticed things that have been amiss, and I need them to tell me.

Audiences give me feedback. In one presentation, I was using my iPhone as a clicker for the slides. That's a nice feature of the app, but I never explained to anyone why I seemed so attached to my phone that I couldn't let go of it even for my talk. "So were you waiting for a phone call?" people wrote in their evaluations. When I watched the video, I could see right away what a distraction the phone was.

The inner critic will tell you far more than you need to know, however. You will hear what you simply cannot do or how you will screw up. And here is what you can tell that naysayer: "Yes, I know I will make mistakes, and they will not hamper me. Yes, I will not be perfect, and that means I can only get better." Even today, whenever I get up in front of people, I get butterflies, but I can control them now and make them flutter in the direction of my choice. It takes a while to train them that way.

The inner critic does have a role, of course. If I were to consider delivering a speech on nuclear physics, I would hope that my inner critic would start screaming at me long before I stood at the lectern. The critic doesn't know when to shut up, however. You might know enough about a topic to deliver a decent speech, but the critic keeps nagging: "Your nose hair is showing. Your tie is crooked. What a nitwit." If you pay too much attention, the prophecies of failure could come true. You get hung up on your shortcomings rather than focusing on your strengths.

The critic isn't one to offer a few words of friendly caution, as in, "Hey, hold on, good fellow. You might wish to read some articles and prepare a bit more before tackling that one just now." No, the inner critic will find less delicate ways of assessing your weaknesses. Sometimes you need to just confront it: "Shut up! Shut up!" You can do that through the "yes, and…" approach of improv. "Yes, I hear what you're saying, and I'm going to do it anyway." The critic may still try to undermine you but not as loudly. You build up self-esteem. You feel confident.

Ready for the Unexpected

When I am doing a presentation, I must be able to adapt because I have no idea what could happen. When I'm booked, I often don't even know what the venue looks like. I once did a presentation for a Fortune 500 company, and the only place they could put me was in a conference room with a table that seated 12—and there were 30 people in attendance. That's not what I had pictured, but I had to adapt.

Seldom are there no uncertainties. You don't know how the weather will be, or traffic conditions, or even whether people will want to hear you. What is the audience's mood? I try to get a feel for that in advance. For example: Is the company planning layoffs? I try to minimize the unknowns, but I know that I still will need to adapt to the unexpected. Otherwise, I might as well just pack up my bags and go home, but who would hire me again?

I once did a one-hour presentation for the Ohio Society of CPAs in Cleveland on technical topics of accounting and auditing updates. It was a room big enough for the 100 people attending. I got there early to set up, and everything was working fine—until it came time to start the presentation. My computer froze. I couldn't get the keynote presentation to work. The screen was locked.

Now, I might have told the audience: "I apologize. I know you're expecting me to start now, but I'm going to need several minutes to get this thing working." However, I had been hired to start and to finish at a specific time. People were counting on an accurate schedule. And so I said: "Well, people, obviously my laptop isn't going to cooperate with me, so here's what we're going to do. You have the materials in front of you, and I'm going to do this without the PowerPoint."

I tried my best to keep the sequence that matched their materials. I'm sure I went off on tangents, but I persevered and finished the presentation, without PowerPoint and within the allotted time. I didn't end early, and I didn't go over. That's part of adapting. If I can't do a one-hour presentation without PowerPoint, I know I'm not prepared. It's a given that things will sometimes go wrong, and it's my job to adapt to that so that the show goes on.

Here's what the inner critic was trying to whisper to me that day: "Boy, you are screwed now, buddy. You're going to look like an idiot. Everyone's going to be laughing at you, and they'll go home and tell everybody you're a loser. And you are. Why didn't you plan for this? Why didn't you have a backup? You jerk."

You can listen to a different voice, instead, the one that says, "You know you can do this." That's the alter ego of the inner critic. That's the voice of improvisation. That's the voice that prevailed as I stood there looking into the frozen screen. "Hey, rest assured, guy, you're prepared. You spent hours on this, so here's an opportunity to prove how well you know this stuff." I found the focus I needed, and I actually enjoyed giving that PowerPointless talk.

Getting Real with the Audience

I do a lot of full-day seminars, and they can be technical or partly technical. The normal slide count for an all-day presentation is about 250. Imagine you are in my shoes, and it is late afternoon, and you have 100 slides still to go and 40 minutes to finish. Instead of focusing on the audience, you're thinking, "I've got to get through all these slides."

I once was preparing for an all-day program on the sexy topic of revenue recognition, and I decided to get rid of 100 slides. I just lopped them off. I figured instead of doing the presentation with 250 slides, I'd do it with 150. "I'm going to trust myself that I'm prepared," I told myself. I would engage the audience and get people talking. I figured that would be a better use of their time than seeing 100 more slides.

We started about 8:30, and by 11 o'clock I was getting a little nervous. The inner critic was saying: "You're going to finish at 2 instead of 4:30, and you can be sure you won't be coming back *here* again." My response: "I'm going to stay focused on the audience, on getting them engaged, on cultivating the topic, on getting people talking."

And when 4:30 came, I still had 15 slides to go.

That change in approach had resulted in a much richer experience on a very dry topic. The reviews were outstanding. Some of the attendees told me they couldn't believe we would get so much dialogue in this type of course. I did it by telling stories about situations and getting people to talk about them. I showed them pictures, which promote interpretation and creative thinking.

I have learned that a speaker needs to have a relationship with the audience, to be real to them, to be someone they would want to talk with. You can be up there with everything in order and all the right slides and steps in place—but is that the kind of tidy package that always works best in dealing with people and with life?

If you have ever taught a child to fish, you probably got a shovel and dug up some worms together, baited the hook, and waited for the bobber to jiggle. You answered the questions as they came naturally, and if the line got stuck in a branch, you figured out together how to solve that problem. Suppose you instead had just taken the child into a dark room, switched on a projector, and said, "This is the process of fishing."

In public speaking, you want to be more than just some officiary who is presenting. You want to involve your audience so that you can get your message to sink in. Whether you are working one on one with somebody or speaking to hundreds of people, the best way to communicate is to establish a relationship.

When the Heads Start Bobbing

I've seen people fall asleep within 15 minutes during an hour-long presentation. Speakers see a lot of heads bobbing, particularly at all-day workshops and seminars. Typically, when people walk out of a presentation like that, about a third of what they heard stays behind them in the room. They don't retain it. Within two weeks they barely remember anything—not even the name of the speaker.

My goal is to get my audiences engaged and have them do a lot of talking, rather than just listening to me go through bullet points in a monotone. I try to create the relationship. I give examples to illustrate the material, and we do some exercises to figure things out together.

I know I'm not going to connect with everybody. I will always have somebody sitting there with that look that clearly projects, "My boss made me come to this." I can't do anything about that person. But as for the rest of them, my goal is to keep their eyes open, to make them laugh, and to stay focused on them while delivering the material.

If I can do that, if I can make that connection, then I feel that I am doing my job well and not just dispensing data to snoozing people. That can be a challenge under the best of circumstances, particularly during the last hour of a long day when I look out at the audience and see what I call Krispy Kreme faces—all glazed over. The mind can only absorb as much as the butt can endure. I'll start breaking into different voices and dialects, trying to keep everyone engaged.

I remember the first time I walked in to teach a college class. It was a night course for older, nontraditional students—a couple dozen faces, all looking at me. I had prepared for that first day, but I didn't know how all this was going to work. The best advice I had been given was this: "Don't ever let them think this is your first day as a teacher. If you do, they will eat you up and spit you out."

Later, when I would hire faculty members and knew it was their first time, I told them the same thing. "Go in there and make them believe you've done this before," I would say. "If they ask you about where you've taught before, avoid specifics and just move off the subject. You're going to be nervous enough as it is."

Yes, that first class of that first term was tough, but that was helpful advice. I came in with technical knowledge and real-life accounting that I could relate to my students, and I think that's what helped with that connection. I wasn't just reading out of a book. I was sharing stories about what it's like to be out there in the working world.

I did have one student who would constantly sleep in class. He fell asleep one day in the front of my class, and I took off my loafers and slammed my shoe on the desk to wake him up. That succeeded in engaging him but only for the moment. So I put him in the back of the class, and he fell asleep there, too. I threw an eraser at him. This was a student who was getting As and Bs in other classes—but he failed mine. I put a premium on connecting with students, on inspiring and motivating. I was determined to have the kind of relationship with them that you cannot have when someone's snoring. No boss is going to accept an employee falling asleep at a meeting. It's a matter of respect. I made it clear to my students: "If you come into my class and fall asleep, you're outta here."

On with the Show

I spoke at the Arizona Society of CPAs accounting conference, arriving about an hour early for my presentation. I've made that my practice so that I can get a feel for the room, make sure all the electronics are working, and do one more review of what I will say.

"Can you go on *now?*" my contact asked me as I walked through the door. "The 9 o'clock speaker isn't here yet—we think he got lost on the way." And so within five minutes I was plugged in, miked up, and speaking. I did a few ice breakers to loosen everybody up, and then we dove into the material.

It was another example demonstrating that you never know what's going to happen. You need to be able to adapt to almost any situation. You must prepare so that you don't miss a beat.

I once heard a story about a gentleman who was giving a presentation and fell off the stage. He apparently misjudged a step. He tucked up and rolled, stood up, and continued his talk. He made it look as if he had done the stunt on purpose.

Now that's what I call thorough preparation for any contingency. The lesson there is to take advantage of your forward momentum, whether you are stumbling literally or figuratively. On with the show.

Chapter 4 Takeaways

⇨ Get out of the casket, and get up to the podium.

⇨ Be engaging and less reliant on
your PowerPoint slides.

⇨ Use "yes, and..." to silence your inner
critic and find the confidence you
need to get your message across.

Seek speaking opportunities within your organization. Remember, most people fear speaking in public, and this is a way to be recognized as a leader. Another suggestion would be to seek out a Toastmasters club in your area or really get outside your comfort zone and attend an improv workshop.

Managing Stress

We complain so much about stress in corporate America and in our daily lives, and some of it is inevitable. Those who rest under the tombstones at the cemetery might be free of stress, depending on whether they're heading north or south in the afterlife, but otherwise we will have our share of it.

Stress can come from so many sources, some of them the daily frustrations of life but others highly troubling, such as major health issues. And stress can be positive as well as negative. You're thinking about getting married—that's positive stress, generally. You're thinking about getting married because you got her pregnant, but you haven't broken the news to her dad—that's negative stress. Why not turn negative stress into positive stress whenever possible? Stress can actually be a motivating force. You might feel inspired, for example, to get a better job and buy an engagement ring before telling the prospective grandpa what's up.

Communication skills will go far in reducing stress. When people feel disrespected or discounted, the stress intensifies. When they feel unheard, they shut down, or they respond with cynicism and distrust or anger—and the situation becomes exponentially worse.

Stress can have value in your life, if you think of it the right way, and if you deal with it in the right way. I have faced many stressful challenges, and I have found that the principles of improv have helped me deal with them.

A Hole in the Heart

When I was 42, I was diagnosed with a hole in my heart.

The news came unexpectedly. The doctor walked into his office, where I was waiting.

"Oh, you're the one," he said and walked back out.

He returned a few minutes later with this news: "You have a hole in your heart."

I had what is called ASD or atrial septal defect. When we are born, we all have a hole between the chambers of the heart that seals itself within days, although sometimes it takes longer. In rare cases, the problem isn't discovered for decades—as was the case with me, of course, since I don't fit in.

I looked at the situation as an opportunity to employ "yes, and..." Yes, I do have a hole in my heart, and if it had been repaired in childhood, I'd have a big scar on my chest because all they could do then was open-heart surgery rather than working through a catheter inserted into my groin.

It was scary, of course. Oh, god, a hole in my heart? I confess that my principles of improvisation took a short hiatus. Instead of saying "yes, and…," I was muttering "oh, crap." Was my son going to grow up without a dad?

The condition came as a big surprise to me, but I knew this was a time for improvising. The surgery was a success. For me, the bigger surprise was that the only place I could get the surgery was at a children's hospital, because this was most commonly a childhood condition. I wondered whether the hospital would have a gown that would fit me. Would everyone run for cover when I walked down the hall?

What does one make of the fact that one's heart has a hole in it? I joke about it with my audiences: "I told my wife, and she cried. I told my mom, and she called a priest. I told my ex-wife, and she was in denial: 'You don't have a heart,' she said."

I'm taking some comedic license there, but it's based on the very real reaction of some of my students—I was a professor at the time—when I told them about my impending surgery.

Comedy comes naturally when you are improvising. Unexpected and surprising associations of ideas—a hallmark of improvisation—are often funny. They are good for comedy but also for stressful situations: the techniques of improv give you the ability to find associations that will work to resolve the problem at hand.

The Challenge of Diabetes

Stress is bad for the heart, as we know, so one would think that reducing stress is a good idea after you find out you have a heart problem, which of course is stressful in itself. To make matters worse, my family background was unknown because I am an adoptee.

So what else might lie in store? A few years later, in 2007, I found out that I'm a diabetic. I realized something was wrong as I was returning from a weekend on Lake Cumberland in Kentucky with Tom Morey, a good friend since our college days. Let's just say my diet that weekend hadn't been the best. There was a lot of liquidity in it. Driving back, I began to experience heart palpitations.

I went to the emergency room. The doctors discovered that my potassium levels were low, prescribed potassium tablets, and told me to check with my cardiologist about the blood work in a week. When the cardiologist office called, I was told the potassium levels had stabilized. Five minutes later, the phone rang again—"Oh, and this is also important," the same person said. "Your blood sugar level is high at 235, and you should get a check for diabetes."

As I hung up, I thought, "Are you kidding me?" First, the hole in the heart, and now diabetes. As it turned out, I wasn't the typical type 2 overweight diabetic—I keep in fairly decent shape—but instead a type 1, which again is usually diagnosed in childhood. At least I'm number one at something.

"You have *what?*" people exclaimed upon hearing of my condition, and I tried the improvisation reaction: "Yes, I have diabetes, and it's not even close to pancreatic cancer of anything of the sort. I'm not going to die tomorrow, and it's not going to slow me down or keep me from chasing my dreams. I just have to manage it."

My mother, who is a nurse, became quite concerned about my blood sugar levels. When she would come for a visit, she would ask me, every time I pricked my finger: "So what's your sugar, son? What's your sugar this time? How much is your sugar?"

"Mom, you're starting to sound like Chris Rock," I told her. It was amazing. My mother turned into Chris Rock.

I do understand everyone's concern, and I take it day by day. I learned to manage carbs and sugar. I changed my diet and cut way back on bread. I eliminated chocolate. I can't have edible panties anymore. Not that big a deal.

People were impressed. "You've got the best attitude for this," my endocrinologist said.

"What other attitude is there to have?" I asked him. If I want to watch my son grow up, and if I want a great life and to grow old with my wife, I don't know any other attitude to take. I'm not going to sit around and feel sorry for myself. Okay, I have a heart problem, and I have diabetes, and, being adopted, who knows what Monty Hall has behind door number three?

I have to adapt to situations that can change by the day because diabetes does not stay constant. Faster than most diabetics, I went from oral meds to an insulin pump. My numbers can be fine for three months and then get out of whack. It can happen weekly or daily. Unless you are experiencing it, it is hard to comprehend. One adapts to keep one's sanity. I try to keep a sensible diet and to take decent care of myself, without living the life of an ascetic. I do have to have a White Castle slider every now and then, just to help the digestive system. That's an old-school probiotic, right there.

When I learned of my condition, I had a choice. I have met some diabetics who live in a fantasy world, believing they need not worry about it. I tend to think such an attitude will put them in the ground someday minus their toes, feet, or legs. Still, I didn't want to live fearfully, either. Some people go into a panic and become obsessed to a point way beyond the necessary attentions and precautions. I chose not to let diabetes affect my life that way.

Picking Up on the Signals

As I have built my business, I have spent a lot of time traveling and standing in front of crowds. I love talking to audiences, but this lifestyle is stressful to the body and can be particularly difficult for a diabetic. My sugar level runs high when I'm on the road, particularly during a presentation—but I told myself I wasn't going to let that stop me from doing what I wanted. I just needed to do some other things differently.

I also need to understand my limits. That's another type of listening that I have fine-tuned. I have to listen to what my body is telling me. If my blood sugar is calling for me to tweak my schedule, I must listen and adapt. And since that's the nature of improv, I was able to apply those skills to yet another facet of life. Improvisation has helped me manage stress so that I can take better care of myself.

When you are aware of the signals, in other words, you will know what to do—and that's true whether you're trying to pick up on the messages that your body is sending you or on the messages that an audience is sending you. It is the awareness itself that plays a major role in reducing stress. Once you know that you will be able to deal with a situation, you develop confidence. You know you will overcome the stress.

A lot of things in my life have been stressful, but as I have encountered them, I have gone with the flow. I have been able to think clearly in chaotic situations through improvisation. The skills of improv clearly are a strength in times of crisis. I listen, assess, and adapt. This also helps to rid drama from my life.

When my blood level is low, my body screams at me. I get the shakes and sweats, and so I need to quickly drink orange juice and take glucose tablets. When the level is high, I can have a hard time putting words together, and it's harder to work with numbers. I have to pause longer than usual to think things through. It's a physical condition that I can easily and quickly remedy, as long as I pick up on those signals and heed them.

If you understand that you can control how your body reacts to a medical condition, then you should also be able to understand that you can control feelings of anxiety when confronted with a new and uncomfortable situation. We all have found ourselves facing appearances we might prefer to avoid, whether we're called into the office or hauled into court or going on a job interview or delivering a speech. Again, you have the power to silence that inner critic's prognostications of impending failure. Tell yourself, "Yes, this feels difficult for me, and I can do it."

Some people find it difficult to adapt. It requires that you listen, focus on the situation, and develop trust, support, and respect. To apply the principles of improvisation, you have to adjust to what others are doing, and they have to adjust to you.

We must do a lot of things that we don't want to tackle. Those tasks become much harder if we cop a bad attitude. "I hate talking to people and networking" will defeat any chance of doing well at such activities. There is a huge difference between "I will do the best I can" and "This is going to fail." If you adopt a better attitude, one that doesn't broadcast defeat, you might actually find that you are doing pretty well. You can feel good about your accomplishment.

People with negative attitudes will just bring you down. I've used improv as my shield to fend off that negativity. Whether your stress results from a physical condition or something else, so much depends on your ability to perceive things positively. You either can see your situation as a challenge and make the most of it, or you can succumb to it and let the stress win.

Worse Than Stage Fright

I once was about to step on stage for a 75-minute presentation to the Ohio Society of CPAs, and five minutes before I was to begin, I could tell my blood sugar was crashing. I quickly downed a Coke, and then I explained to someone from the society what was going on.

"Listen," I told her, "I need you in this room. If I pass out, you need to call an ambulance. I need you to call 911. I'll know in time to give you a sign, and if I do, then call somebody because I'm going down like a sack of potatoes."

"Pete, I think maybe you'd better not do this…"

"That's all right," I said. "If I get through ten minutes, I'll be all right. But I'm just putting a contingency plan in place here. It's time to start—and it's important to start on time."

For a bit, I was as white as Casper the Friendly Ghost. My face was the color of a crisp, white dress shirt.

The room was set up for tables of eight, and I tend to walk around to promote connectivity with the audience. This time I kept to the front of the room, and I was sweating and having some difficulty talking. Those people in the first few tables must have thought, "That's the worst case of stage fright I've ever seen." Or if they had seen me talk before, maybe they thought, "I wonder what he's on?"

It was surreal, but after ten minutes, I could tell that I was getting my feet back, and I got through the whole 75 minutes. Let's just say I got home, and I didn't get out of bed for about a day and a half. My endocrinologist explained that to get me through the crisis, my adrenaline levels had risen so high that I had nothing left in the tank.

But I hadn't panicked. I refused to tell myself that I couldn't do it. I didn't accept a late start—I had been hired to start and stop at specific times. I wanted to make it clear that I was willing and able to give 110 percent—and that's what improvisation allows you to do. It lets you operate clearly without panicking in chaotic situations. You know you can figure a way out. With those principles, I feel that I can adapt to almost anything in business and in life.

Down a Different Path

For a long time, I never held a job longer than four years or so. Back in the day, that was considered job hopping. Now it's considered the mark of somebody who has a lot of skill sets in a lot of environments who can bring a lot to an organization. How times have changed.

I remember when I was downsized, reorganized, restructured, laid-off, fired from Victoria's Secret Catalogue. That was extremely stressful. It came on the same day that I had gotten a really solid job review. A few hours later, the boss called me back into her office. "We've decided to disband your department and your team," she said, "so your job has been eliminated."

I had never been fired in my life. I did my best to adapt—but then I was asked to stay on for a week or so to help with the transition. When I left for good the next Friday, knowing I wouldn't be coming back, I felt as if I were in shock.

I had a three-month severance package. I visited a counselor for Right & Associates. They were going to teach me "how to fish," as they say—that is, how to find my next job. I went into that office on Monday morning and looked out the window at the view of Interstate 270, which goes around Columbus. "I have nowhere to be today," I thought. "It's a Monday, but it's not like I'm on vacation. I don't have a job." The counselor was talking to me, but I wasn't listening. I wasn't focused. All I could think of was that I didn't have a job, and I was in crisis mode.

A few days later, I started coming out of that fog. "This is a good thing for you," I told myself. "When one door closes, another one opens. Who knows where this will lead? At your next appointment, Pete, you will focus and listen. You will be in the moment, looking for opportunities. You won't panic. You have your three months of severance pay, and you can figure this out. This is a journey, a different path."

I thought about what my biggest complaints at Victoria's Secret Catalogue had been. I had put in 50 to 65 hours each and every week. I had worked there four years, but that's like 28 years in a dog's life, and I worked in women's underwear. (Okay, that last one was an upside.) But I wouldn't have to deal with the stresses anymore. I just needed to figure out what I could do next. I thought about those three letters behind my name, CPA, and felt a sense of reassurance that something would come my way. I could teach it, or I could practice it, if need be—and I could become better.

I felt a sense of calm. Perhaps it came from the professional safety net that I had put in place. Someone had once told me, "Pete, I think you'd be a good teacher," and I kept that in mind. At my three-month mark, though, I needed a job, and so I became a company's headhunter for a while. I ended up applying for an adjunct position at Franklin University in Columbus—and the next thing I knew, that's where I was. I was a professor of accounting.

I think again how things might have turned out if I had not been fired from Victoria's Secret Catalogue and if I had not gone into teaching. Where I am today is largely a result of working at the university and learning all about curriculum design and delivery of courses. Had I not found myself in those circumstances, I don't think my journey would have taken this direction. That's why I believe it is so important to listen—not just to people, not just to one's body but to the environment in which you find yourself. What is your current situation telling you about your abilities and your goals?

Losing a job can be a blow to the ego, not to mention a blow to the wallet. The stress can feel unbearable, but then a door opens and your life changes. In order to see that door open, you have to listen, focus, and adapt without panic. Panic can send you into a freefall.

Humor As a Healer

I once did a presentation on "humor at work" for an accounting firm in Dayton, Ohio. I explained that when we laugh, our bodies release "endolphins"—you know, those playful fish that go leaping and diving through the bloodstream to help us fight stress and anxiety and depression.

Later, as I read the written evaluations of my presentation, five attendees—yes, five—informed me that dolphins are mammals, not fish. "Mr. Margaritis," one of them wrote, "you should know better." Let me emphasize here that I am not reinforcing the stereotype that accountants are humorless. They hardly need my help.

So many workplaces seem devoid of humor. I ask my audiences, "When was the last time your coworkers burst out into laughter and it wasn't at your expense?" Stress is the reason for all that office ennui. People are in survival mode, just trying to get through till quitting time. In fact, when you're facing a tough deadline or enduring an impossible task, the last thing you probably want to hear is some joker saying, "Hey, did you hear the one about the priest, the rabbi, and Bill Clinton walking into a bar?" You want to rip their tonsils out.

A regular dose of laughter, however, reduces stress. It has proven health benefits. Researchers have found that stress constricts the arteries and vessels and reduces blood flow to the brain, resulting in costly mistakes of judgment. There is truth, therefore, to the old saying that laughter is the best medicine. It loosens us up. It has also been found to bolster the immune system. When we're stressed out, we get sicker quicker, and we make others sick. Productivity plummets. Laughter is the proven antidote, and it comes naturally when the company culture is conducive to it. A bit of levity need not be seen as evidence that the employees are goofing off again.

Chapter 5 Takeaways

⇨ Communication skills will go far in reducing stress, especially when you use the method of "yes, and…"

⇨ Remember to listen to understand versus listening to respond to help combat stress.

⇨ Fight the Debbie Downers—those people who have a black cloud following them at all times—with doses of respect, "yes, and…," and the right attitude.

What is stressful in your life today? Is it positive stress or negative stress? Adopt a way from this chapter to help deal with your stress.

chapter 6

Straight Talk

Lincoln's Gettysburg Address
(revised for modern corporate audiences)

> *Fourscore and seven years ago, our stakeholders brought forth on this continent a new nation, conceived in liberty and dedicated to the value proposition that all men are created on a net-net basis.*

> *Now we are operating in the space of a great civil war, testing whether that nation, or any nation so conceived and so dedicated, can add value while moving forward. We are met on a great battlefield of that war. We have come to dedicate a portion of that field as a final resting place for those who here gave their lives that that nation might experience a game changer. It altogether is what it is.*

But, from the 10,000-foot view, we cannot dedicate, we cannot consecrate, we cannot hallow this ground. The brave men, living and dead, who struggled here, have consecrated it far above our poor power to add or detract. In the big picture, people will little note nor long misremember what we say here but can never literally forget what they did here. It is for us the living, rather, to be robust about pushing the envelope for the unfinished new paradigm which they who fought here have thus far so nobly advanced. At the end of the day, it is rather for us to be here dedicated to the great task remaining before us; that from these honored dead will come a win-win for that cause for which they gave 110 percent in their last full measure of devotion; that we here proactively resolve that these dead shall not have died in vain; that this nation, under God, shall see the glass as half full and have a new out-of-the-box freedom; and that the intellectual capital of the people, by the people, for the people shall not perish from the earth.

First, let me offer my apologies to President Lincoln, but folks today just don't talk the same way they did in his day, so I have taken the liberty of translating his famous address into terms that would be recognized in boardrooms everywhere.

I recently was in Vancouver, British Columbia, and I was doing a session on communicating in the workplace. We talked about buzzwords and technical jargon, such as "reaching out" and "the 10,000-foot view" and "back of the envelope" and so many others. I pointed out how empty they are. There's nothing to them.

When somebody is just using a bunch of buzzwords and jargon, then the "listeners," if you can call them that, aren't going to pay as much attention. When you are subjected to a barrage of vapid words, you tend to tune the speaker out and wait for your chance to say something. If we would just use simpler words and real language, more people would care about what we have to say.

I was talking about buzzwords with my old college friend Tom Morey, with whom I try to spend a weekend every year in Kentucky. We spend a lot of time on his boat, and we eat lots of good food, and we sample the various bourbons that we tend to bring with us. He's a sales rep for a pharmaceutical company. Our conversation at a recent meeting somehow drifted to the rampant growth of meaningless words. After the weekend, we exchanged a series of text messages using as many corporate buzzwords as we could, just for laughs.

That exchange spurred me to write a blog and article titled "Eliminate Corporate Buzzwords". Here's what I wrote:

> *I have called this meeting so we can "reach out" to our customers to provide them with a "value proposition" based on industry "best practices." The "bottom line" is that we "have to go the extra mile" to provide an "amazing" "customer experience" so we can have a "win-win" situation. I need everyone to "think outside the box" and go through the "ideation" process so we can "leverage" our position and provide efficient "bandwidth" so that "at the end of the day" we can "incentivize" you on a "net-net" basis. "Spitball" ideas with anyone on the team "offline." We all need to be "teed up" on this initiative because our "stakeholders" and the company need to "be singing from the same hymnal." Let's do some "back of the envelope" calculations and focus for now on "the low-hanging fruit."*

It is important that we have our "talking points" aligned, and I will "circle back" with each of you to "level set" our strategy so that this does not turn into a "train wreck." Any questions? Good, let's all go "the extra mile" on this initiative.

Does this sound familiar? Are you scratching your head now as much as you do when you experience this at work? What happened to a simpler way of speaking? Here are some buzzwords and what I think of when I hear them:

- **10,000-foot view**: I don't know any of the details.

- **Back of the envelope**: We are out of legal pads.

- **Benchmarking**: My photo is on a bus stop bench.

- **Bio-break**: I am in buzzword hell if I can't even say "restroom."

- **Circle back**: Circle back mountain.

- **Emotional leakage**: Looks like a going concern. I better get a pair of Depends.

- **In the loop**: I am going to hang myself if I hear another corporate buzzword.

- **Intellectual capital**: The opposite of Congress.

- **Low-hanging fruit**: Going commando.

- **Space**: The final frontier.

- **Stakeholders**: For those who like corn-on-the-cob holders.

- **Value proposition**: Negotiating with a prostitute.

Let's put my blog paragraph in a simple and understandable format:

I have called this meeting to begin the conversation of how we can improve our customer service. Everyone in this room has thoughts on this topic, and we want to hear them so we can determine which to implement. The team with the best idea will win $10,000. Generate as many ideas as possible. We want quantity. We will determine quality afterward. This is a high priority initiative from the board of directors. As part of this process, what little things can we start doing today to improve our customer service? I will be meeting with each team this next week to gather their ideas, and we all will meet in two weeks with our strategy. I thank you in advance for your hard work.

We went from 185 words down to 123 words—a 33 percent reduction in words and a 100 percent improvement in clarity. I'm starting a campaign to eliminate buzzwords at work, and you don't even have to dump ice water over your head. Are you in?

You may have a buzzword that you particularly despise, and chances are it's somewhere in the parody above—or in my buzzspeak rendition of Mr. Lincoln's immortal words. These hollow expressions take the place of real thought. I'm thinking that if the Great Emancipator had been a product of today's corporate culture, his address would have been mind-numbing.

In my 20-odd years in the CPA profession, I have observed that communication skills are not one of the sought-out traits. Some accountants possess those skills, but a majority of them do not. It's as if they were saying to clients, "My firm is too big to meet your needs. Let me find someone else to help you." Phone calls and emails go unreturned, and the possibilities fade away.

A Lesson in the Snowflakes

Sometimes as an icebreaker I ask everyone in my audience to pull out a blank sheet of paper and tell them that they are to listen carefully and follow my instructions to the T but that they cannot ask any questions. "Fold the paper in half," I say, and I give them a moment to comply. Then: "Tear off the bottom right corner. Fold the paper in half again. Tear off the bottom right corner. Fold it in half one more time, and this time chew off the bottom left corner."

Then I ask everyone to unfold their sheet of paper, and I walk around the room examining them. Whether I have a crowd of 20 or 100, I rarely find any two alike. Like real snowflakes, each is unique.

"People, help me understand something," I ask. "I gave you instructions for each step. So why isn't every snowflake exactly the same?"

"Well," they often respond, "you didn't give us detailed instructions."

"You're right, I didn't." I agree. "Some of what I said was open to interpretation." I pause to let them think about it. How could I expect the same results, they wonder, if I didn't explain which direction to fold or how much to tear off or how big a bite to chew?

"Has something like that ever happened to you?" I ask. "Have your employees ever done something that bore little resemblance to what you expected? What they heard wasn't what you had requested—and that might well have been because you didn't take the extra minute or two to give them detailed instructions and make sure they completely understood. You didn't explain yourself, and you didn't let them question you."

"As a result, you feel frustrated or angry, and the employees are upset and don't understand what they did wrong. Stress levels balloon. You wonder whether the employees have a clue, and the employees see you as ineffective, and all of you are sharing your impressions with your colleagues. Office morale plummets. Everything seems to take more time."

That's the root of a lot of workplace tension. It happens all the time. Poor communication leads to increased stress. It comes from not understanding what someone is saying, from not knowing what they want, and from not giving sufficient directions. People complain about their long workdays, but the days can seem so much longer when we fail to effectively communicate as we delegate.

As a result, the managers may cease to delegate at all and just do the work themselves, feeling it's the only way it will be done right. And in such a tense atmosphere, the staff may feel intimidated and hold back from asking the very questions that will get them the information they need to do excellent work.

Negotiating Successfully

Conducting a successful negotiation requires six major skills—and those skills are really based on the principles of improvisation.

1. Take your ego off the table.

2. **Respect** the other party.

3. Be in the moment (**focus**).

4. **Listen** to the other party's needs and wants.

5. **Adapt** to the situation.

6. **Yes, and...**

I think using these steps can help to take emotions off the table. When emotion gets involved in negotiations, things can go awry. We are more likely to succeed in negotiations when both parties can envision a common goal. In this kind of negotiation, the parties are willing to compromise. The attitude should be, "I may have to give up something, but when we are done we'll both come away feeling successful." Some people—not me!—would call that a "win-win." That's not exactly the tack that Congress tends to take, which is more "I win, you lose." No compromise. That's how toddlers often act: demanding and whining if they don't get their way.

At a recent conference, a participant commented that he had discovered that the power of "yes, and..." really does work, especially with negotiations. He was on a nonprofit board for a youth sports league and wanted to communicate that he felt their facility needed a new floor. He expected to hear a lot of rejection because it involves change, which people tend to resist.

So he did do his homework. He talked to people about the project and collected all the negatives on why they felt it would never work. When it came time to make the pitch to the board, he knew all of the "yes, buts..." He turned each of them into a "yes, and..." "Well yes, and this is how we're going to do it." "Yes, and this is how we'll implement." "Yes, and this is what it's going to take." "Yes, and this will be the cost."

He was amazed at how that defused the negativity. "Yes, and..." allowed them to see the benefits that he was bringing to the table. And ultimately, the deal was accepted and implemented.

He said he hadn't realized he was using the power of "yes, and..." He didn't know about that concept at the time—except instinctively. He was finding a point of agreement and extending the argument further to see what would happen with it. By doing his homework, he understood what the pushback would be. He was able to put aside his ego—which wasn't that large anyway—and emphasize respect for the other party. He respected their positions and understood where they were coming from.

By being prepared, he was able to be in the moment, focused and listening to what they were truly saying and applying it to what he had learned. That is what allowed him to steer and adapt during the conversation in the manner that helped him to win. He had validated the power of improvisation.

Successful people all intuitively do this. They just don't necessarily realize that they are using improvisation in their daily lives. Skillful negotiation is actually fun, many people find, and that makes it all the more motivating.

"Time and emotion," Anthony K. Tjan wrote in a recent Harvard Business Review blog, "are the two things most often wasted during a negotiation. We simply spend too much time on items that don't really matter, because we let our emotions override any semblance of logic."

We tend to react emotionally and negatively to any points of negotiation that oppose our own agenda. And that wastes time. When our goals for a negotiation are so firmly anchored that we cannot budge, it becomes hard to see any common goal as a solution. Instead, emotions kick in, and egos inflate—and we cease to listen.

To succeed in negotiations, we need to take the egos off the table and drop our agendas long enough to truly listen—and with respect for all involved. I'm not necessarily talking about formal negotiations around a conference table. This is the way to success in the daily negotiations of life and career—during a chat with the boss or with one's spouse, or with a child. This is the kind of straight talk we can cultivate that truly will make the biggest difference.

Chapter 6 Takeaways

⇨ Eliminate corporate buzzwords from your vocabulary to invite listening from the other party.

⇨ The six major skills in negotiating are: take your ego off the table, respect the other party, be in the moment, listen to the other party's needs and wants, adapt to the situation, and "yes, and..."

Spend the extra minute or two to be sure that the other party understands the instructions you have given. Make a list of corporate buzzwords that you use daily, and find substitute, nonjargon words as their replacement.

Business Development

While having lunch with a businessman recently, I picked his brain for information that my audiences might find helpful. I wanted to know the sorts of things that kept him up at night. I asked him questions and listened intently.

"You know, Pete," he said at one point, "what I really wish is that my people would do what you are doing right now."

"What do you mean?"

"Well, I wish they would be good listeners and ask the right questions and probe for information," he said. "I wish they would get engaged with people. You know, that's all part of developing business. You have to be able to sit across the table from someone."

I think that's one of the challenges that accounting firms with younger staff are having. Inexperienced salespeople are failing to ask questions and are only pitching what their company has to offer.

In our business dealings, we often are guilty of just not listening. We come to the table with an agenda—a new product, a new service—and wait while a prospect or existing client tells us what's going on with his or her business. At some point, that person will pause—and we pounce.

It takes practice, and it takes work to set aside your own agenda so that you can truly hear what others are going through and how you might join together for your common benefit. In building a business, you want to either attract new clients or retain existing ones—and the first step is to understand your audience.

Business development requires dealing with those who may not share your views or approach. You need to know people's communication and personality styles in order to build effectively. In a public accounting firm or in any organization, you are in the people business—and all people don't speak the language of business in the manner that accountants do.

For example, when you say the word "depreciation" to non-accountants, they might first think about the value they lose when they drive a new car off the lot. The accountant, by contrast, is thinking about "a systematic allocation of an asset over time." It's a different language. Each of us needs to adapt to how others communicate, and we need to let them know our own style.

In understanding our differences, we need to remember the differences between left-brain people (the analytical types like accountants, engineers, and actuaries who prefer coloring inside the lines and being in the box) and right-brain people (the creative types who tend to color outside the lines and who, as a matter of fact, have no idea where the box is).

A number of tests can help us to understand the personality and communication styles of others, including the Myers-Briggs, DISC, and HBDI. Myers-Briggs is probably the most recognized of these. If you have ever taken the Myers-Briggs test, you may remember you got a four-letter result, such as ENTJ or INTP. I came out as SLOW, and so I took the test again and became a BORE.

On the HBDI test, the results indicated that I had a whole brain, which surprised my parents and most of my friends. But what this test really showed was that neither side of my brain is dominant and that both sides are fighting for attention. I have a very creative side, and I have an analytical side, believe it or not—and that's one reason that I feel that I am an Accidental Accountant™.

The DISC model has four quadrants: dominance, influence, steadiness, and conscientiousness. Influence and steadiness are on the right side of the brain, and dominance and conscientiousness are on the left side. (Just as a side note, successful sitcoms often include a character from each of those quadrants, because the resulting friction tends to be funny.)

Let's take a look at people in each of those quadrants.

Dominance

These are the drivers among us. They are competitive, decisive, independent, determined, and results-oriented. They want control and admiration. They also tend to be domineering, impatient, and poor listeners. They dislike disorganization and wasted time. They don't think you should bring your feelings into work. They can be hot tempered. Some see them as bullies. People in this category could include Donald Trump, Mark Cuban, and Jerry Seinfeld. Why might people in this category be considered poor listeners? It's because they are the deciders, audiences explain to me. They have rendered the decision, and anyone else's words are wasting precious oxygen.

Influence

These are the cheerleader types who want to do what they love without being confused by the facts. These people are optimistic, animated, persuasive, imaginative, and enthusiastic. They are good communicators. They love having fun, being the center of attention, and receiving applause. They are dreamers. However, they may talk too much, overwhelming others with information. They have short attention spans. What was I talking about? Squirrels...oh yeah, I remember. They don't like being alone, and they don't like structure. At their worst, they tend to be disorganized and miss deadlines. In this group, you might include a lot of salespeople, as well as people such as Oprah Winfrey and, to revisit *Seinfeld*, the character Elaine.

Steadiness

These are the "can't we all just get along and work together" people. They worry about whether others are okay. They are friendly, reliable, and supportive, like a Labrador retriever. They are patient and diplomatic. They want everyone to like them and obsess if someone doesn't. They are very concerned about personal relationships and harmony in the workplace but tend to be overly sensitive, conformist, and lacking in time boundaries. They won't tell you what they think; instead, they will tell you what you want to hear— which can be a dangerous trait. They don't like to be rushed, they don't want to be alone, and they avoid conflict when possible. You would never find them watching *The Jerry Springer Show*. At their worst, they tend to be indecisive, easily overwhelmed, and miss deadlines. You find these types in human resources departments. Examples might include Mister Rogers or Kramer from the *Seinfeld* world.

Conscientiousness

These are the thinkers. They want to get it right all the time, and they want to be efficient, thorough, accurate, and careful. They are disciplined and love solving problems and researching. This group tends to be very critical and picky. They don't like disorganization or surprises. At their worst, they are rigid, argumentative, and stubborn. These are accountants, engineers, actuaries. If you are a fan of *The Big Bang*

Theory, the character Sheldon Cooper is the quintessential conscientiousness individual. On *Seinfeld*, it's George Costanza.

Among these personality types, friction will naturally arise because these are people with opposite outlooks. Still, you must work well with all types, since every group contains people in each category. How do we connect, how do we adapt, to someone who is not like us?

- To connect with those who are in the dominant quadrant, be direct, be specific, and offer multiple solutions. Remember, they are the decider. If you give them only one option, it's more than likely going to fail, or it can become their idea instead of yours.

- To connect with those who are in the influence quadrant, be enthusiastic and positive, and avoid details. Put things in a way that they can relate to. I have often heard accountants complain that the salespeople never get their expense reports in on time. My solution would be to point out to those salespeople that they file early for their tax refund so that the government doesn't get to use their money any longer than necessary, so they should submit their expense report to the company for a similar reason.

- To connect with those who are in the steadiness quadrant, engage in small talk, ask a lot of questions, and be informal, as if talking with a friend. Just don't let them suck away your time and extend your workday. You need to be respectful but firm about managing the conversation. Let them know you appreciate the chatting, but it's time to get down to business.

- And for those of us who are in the conscientiousness quadrant, we need to communicate to people in the other three that we would like to focus on just the facts, please, so that we can get organized.

It all starts with respect. Communication goes two ways, so the better we understand others—including their pet peeves and their hot buttons, their likes and dislikes—the better we will get along. Once again it's all about listening carefully to what people need and want, adapting readily to the situation, and taking your own agenda off the table.

A Secret to Business Success

By helping us understand the needs and wants of clients and customers, the principles of improvisation are a powerful tool for developing business.

In the world of improv, people talk a lot about commitment. You need to be fully committed to your character. If you're going to be the tree, be the best tree that you can be. If you're going to be a crazy game show host, be the craziest. Be fully committed to that character.

That's a lesson for businesses, too. If you don't have the passion for what you're selling, then you're not going to sell it. Suppose you're trying to sell those clickers that speakers use in their presentations. "Hey, would you like to buy this clicker? It helps in presentations, and it has a couple of useful buttons. What do you say?" You can expect to hear a resounding no. You haven't shown passion or energy. You haven't communicated that this is the world's best clicker, that everyone should have one, and what your clicker has meant to you personally.

It's hard to fake enthusiasm, but a good salesman can do it. Enthusiasm is what sells. The customer is looking for passion behind the words. In my nontechnical presentations, people can see my passion. I get great reviews for my technical talks, too, and I think it's because my passion for the soft skills flows over to my presentation of the hard ones. I make dry stuff fun. Most technical talks are delivered in a dry, monotone manner.

When somebody contacts me about the possibility of doing a presentation, I ask a lot of questions. "What are the issues you are facing? What kinds of presentations have you been offering, on what topics?" And a key one: "What is your expectation after the two hours that I present? What behaviors are you trying to change? Which issues should I address, and what do you wish me to stay away from?" So, in essence, I try to customize my presentation. I don't want it to be canned, particularly for the nontechnical topics.

A presenter has to understand the audience. Who's in that audience? What are their needs and wants, and what behaviors are they trying to change, modify, or enhance? One cannot succumb to tunnel vision or complacency. We have to stop and think about what differentiates us from the competition.

Chapter 7 Takeaways

⇨ Make better connections with others by identifying where they fall in the DISC model and adapt your style to meet theirs.

⇨ Park your agenda, and listen to understand the needs and wants of your client or customer.

⇨ "Yes, and..." will help in guiding the conversation to uncover the needs and wants in order to provide solutions.

Go back and review the four quadrants of the brain according to the DISC model. List people that you know in the quadrant that you think they fall in. The next time you come in contact with a person, see if you can devise a way to make a better connection.

Cultivating Creativity

S everal colleagues were brainstorming about ways that they might increase their company's profitability. They tossed out some possibilities and mulled over the relative advantages and disadvantages.

"I have an idea!" one of them said after a long pause. "I think we should poison our competitor's sales team!"

I presume that gentleman's comment, as related to me by a participant in one of my workshops, was meant in jest. But I concede there is a limit to how far you can go when declaring that "no idea is a bad idea." We want to stay away from murder and miscellaneous mayhem.

For the most part, though, you should not dismiss any idea too quickly as unworthy. A questionable idea often can be developed into a much better one. Instead of poisoning the competitor's sales team, for example, maybe you could consider whom you might poach from it.

Creativity is the foundation of innovation. I look at creativity as the generation of ideas, the more the better. In creativity workshops, I explain that we should not worry that an idea might be bad, because in any case it will lead to a better idea. So whatever is in your head, let it out—within reason—even if it doesn't seem the best of ideas. Bad ideas lead to good ideas. No idea leads to nothing.

Don't Poison the Pool

For creativity to surface, we need to silence that inner critic. You don't feel particularly creative when you hear the critic harping about your stupid ideas. It's important when brainstorming to let all ideas rise. You can narrow them down later. At this stage, don't poison the pool of creativity.

Once the inner critic shuts up, people will feel free to say what they wish—that is, if the atmosphere is conducive to such expression. It's important to establish some rules for brainstorming. If 30 people in an accounting firm—staff, management, junior managers, and partners—gather in a room to come up with new ideas, it is likely that some will feel timid about speaking up. They will wonder what the partners might think of them. You therefore need to put a firm rule in place: "Never mind your rank for now. What's said in this room stays in this room. It will not be used to judge anybody."

This doesn't happen overnight, but if the leadership encourages the generation of ideas, some of them are bound to produce impressive results. Not all the ideas are going to work, no matter how much product testing and field work a company conducts. Some ideas will go nowhere, but if you have no ideas, you certainly will go nowhere.

Years ago, Anheuser-Busch wanted a new marketing campaign and needed to create a commercial for the Super Bowl. I imagine they gathered the best and brightest marketers into a room to brainstorm. Some man or woman in the back of the room—there's always someone in the back of the room—stands up and says, "I have an idea, why don't we put three frogs on lily pads in a swamp and have them say, *Bud... Weis... Er.*"

What do three frogs on lily pads have to do with beer? I am sure someone in that room must have said, "Yes, but that's the stupidest idea I've ever heard, what do frogs have to do with beer?" A different reaction: "Yes, and maybe lizards and other creatures would be good for selling stuff, too!" The concept of "yes, and..." keeps the conversation and inspiration flowing.

Creative Clustering

It's that "yes, and..." principle of improv that will get those ideas out of people's heads. I use a technique called mind mapping and clustering. If you have an objective, think about things associated with that objective. Some will be attributes, and some will be details.

Let's say you have been asked to write an essay on "what I do on Saturdays," but you have writer's block. You don't know where to begin. Clustering helps you to lay it all out. You might think of things such as mowing the grass, kids' soccer, housework, playing golf, or fixing a leaky faucet. As you think about them and write them down, you will be able to group them: some are chores, for example, and others are sporting events. Those are attributes, which the details describe.

This is a very simple example, but the concept works well when dealing with complex matters. From a creative perspective, once the mind is able to see the details and attributes, it often will connect the dots in new ways to produce novel associations and ideas.

Think of it this way: if you were writing a book, your objective would be the title. The attributes would be the chapters. And the details would be the supporting information within each chapter.

If your objective is to open a new restaurant, you start by considering some of the details and attributes of what you anticipate you will be doing. What type of food do you want to serve? Do you want to open it in the city or the countryside? Is there a particular theme you want to emphasize? What will be your reputation for service? As you imagine your restaurant, you will be able to list dozens of details, and they will readily cluster into attributes.

You just connect the dots. Perhaps you want to open a Greek restaurant on the beach with a rain forest theme and so-so service. (Or perhaps not.) Whatever your dream, you can quickly create a specific picture from a general concept through this technique of mind mapping.

It goes back to associations. You take two things that may not seem to go together and put them together. That's the essence of creativity. Suppose you have a hot dog in one hand and a stick in the other. Put them together, fry it in batter, and voila! You have a corndog. A stroke of creative genius, I would say.

More Than Facts and Figures

The inner critic will try to stop all that creative nonsense, but the powers of improvisation will open the doors to the possibilities. Whether you are mind mapping or brainstorming, the point is to keep the ideas percolating. Creativity arises from the free association of words and ideas, and no search engine can produce that for you.

You need more than just the facts. You want to discover relationships between them. Accountants are very facts-oriented people. The challenge is to get them to see that there's more to their profession than just the facts and figures.

When I do a creativity workshop and ask those attending whether they think of themselves as creative, maybe one or two people will raise a hand.

"You weren't born and raised in this profession, were you?" I ask the group. "I bet you started out doing other things. You're like me."

And they often agree. "I think I'm an Accidental Accountant™, too," I regularly hear after my presentations. "I was a social worker before I got into this"—or some other career path that calls for people-oriented, right-brain thinking.

I show them ways that they can be creative. It's a big challenge to silence the inner critic and learn to express yourself. Often their mindset is that they really do just want the facts, and they can be very introverted and reluctant to share their thoughts. That's quite an impediment to creative thinking.

Every time I've done a creativity workshop, whether it's for an organization or accounting firm or as a general seminar, there's a strange thing called laughter that happens. I see accountants having fun—while also coming up with ideas and solutions. I think they kind of amaze themselves. Unfortunately, as they leave the seminar, it's as if they are putting their accountant suits back on.

It's as if they are saying, "Okay, that was fun, I get it. But I could never do that out there." I truly believe that if they are to succeed, they have to do it out there. They have to deal with people. Accounting is numbers, yes, but those numbers represent someone's life's work and dreams and desires. You have to get those numbers right, and accuracy is essential, but you also need to know what those numbers stand for. Otherwise, they're just digits in the ether.

That's what ties it all together, the fact that we're human beings on a common journey, trying to accomplish something together. That's why we need to let creative ideas bubble up where they will. If you keep bursting those bubbles, you lose so much opportunity.

It's All in the Approach

Good leaders inspire and encourage the expression of creativity. They recognize that their people have a lot of ideas. "Tell me what's on your mind. Tell me what you're thinking. Let's get it out," they say. What comes out might be a bit rough, but with a little polishing it could be beautiful. Successful leaders value that creativity muscle. They get the most from their people without deflating them.

What is the point of asking people what they are thinking if you are going to beat them up for what they say? That's not leadership. That's bullying, and it happens a lot. It's deflating, demotivating, demoralizing, and humiliating. Criticism strikes people down, and they clam up. And some people wither without affirmation.

That's not to say we shouldn't challenge one another to reach for greater heights. But it's all in the approach. We can be agreeable in our disagreements so that we work together toward solutions, in the spirit of cooperation rather than confrontation. Whenever possible, why not find some point of accord and then branch out from there? Instead of competitors, you become collaborators: "Yes, and have you ever thought about it this way, though?" The goal is to examine and explore and develop.

Many people, somewhere deep inside, feel a sense of insecurity that perhaps they don't know enough. That's why criticism feels so sharp to them and halts the conversation. "Yes, and..." helps to affirm and reassure so that ideas can blossom.

Chapter 8 Takeaways

⇨ Creativity is about generating ideas
by silencing your inner critic.

⇨ Bad ideas lead to good ideas—
no ideas lead to nothing.

⇨ Organizational status is left out of the room
when brainstorming. Respect everyone's ideas,
and what is said in the room stays in the room.

Conduct a 15-minute brainstorming session with your team on any objective at hand. See how many ideas you can come up with. Put a jar in the middle of the table, and if someone says "yes but…" or "that's crazy" or "we can't do that" or "that's a stupid idea," they need to contribute a dollar. See how quickly the conversation changes in a positive way.

Leveraging Your Leadership

There's a scene in the movie *Remember the Titans* where Denzel Washington, playing a football coach at a high school facing the racial tensions of integration, has a talk with his team after taking them on a run through the woods at the Gettysburg battlefield.

"This is where they fought the Battle of Gettysburg," he tells them. "Men died right here on this field, fighting the same fight that we're still fighting amongst ourselves today. This green field right here was painted red, bubbling with the blood of young boys, hot lead pouring right through their bodies."

"If we don't come together, right now, on this hallowed ground, then we, too, will be destroyed. Just like they were."

"I don't care if you like each other or not, but you will respect each other. And maybe we'll learn to play this game like men."

He was saying, in essence, that a team can achieve only if each member can achieve respect for the others. Whether we like one another isn't as important as whether we give one another support—and that's as true in the workplace or in a family as it is on a sports team. You might not like your neighbor or wish to chat with him over the fence, but if you have reached any level of maturity you aren't going to heckle and disrespect him and his family.

Spotlight on Others

Throughout this book, we have been defining the components of effective leadership as we have examined various topics such as communication, networking, public speaking, managing stress, and creativity. Leaders need to develop their people and enhance their talents and make them look good—and when they do so, the spotlight eventually will shine on themselves.

That development must include more than technical skills. Good leaders recognize the importance of respect, trust, and support. When you are building a team, you need to uphold those principles. Unless the leaders are having those critical conversations with the staff, they are not managing people. They are simply managing processes.

Improvisation is all about positive attitude and outlook. Successful leaders possess the skills of improv. They need a variety of qualities such as the ability to build a team, to inspire and motivate others to adopt their vision, and to accept the risk associated with their decisions.

In today's business climate, successful leaders must be able to communicate their vision and their ideas, while adapting to the changing business landscape. They must be able to move forward even within an arena of uncertainty. Successful leaders and improvisers process information quickly, and they are creative, innovative, and willing to see different perspectives. They strive to make their teammates look good.

I sometimes see a dismissive look in people's eyes when I mention the word "improv," as if to say, "What are you trying to sell me here?" They soon learn that improvisation involves a lot more than comedy. Leaders must respect, trust, support, listen, focus, and adapt. They need that "yes, and..." attitude. In building the team, you must encourage colleagues to regard one another in the way that the coach pointed out so poignantly in *Remember the Titans*.

It's often said that God gave us two ears and one mouth for a reason. We are built for listening, so we should do it. The most successful leaders listen to their people. They listen to their environment. They can forget their own agenda long enough to adapt. They are 100 percent focused and able to take a conversation in creative directions. They don't shut things down with "yes, but..."

Any leader will encounter trying circumstances and confusing situations, and the principles of improv provide clarity. Making tough decisions is the leader's job, and those decisions might not be popular. Sometimes ego gets in the way. It can be easy to forget that leadership is about the team and making others look good. A leader must be able to mentor, coach, groom, and provide others with the resources for success.

Each of the actors on *Whose Line Is It Anyway?* has a pretty big ego. But each knows his proper place. Everyone wants to deliver the word or the line that gets the biggest laugh. But at times, it's not your turn. At times, whatever you are about to say would not be appropriate and would kill the scene. Instead, you need to help set somebody else up in order to make the ensemble look better. You need to be able to drop your ego.

Changing the Conversation

In my mind, that's successful leadership—making others around you look better. At the opening retreat after I was installed as chairman of the Ohio Society of CPAs executive board, I began by introducing the concepts of improvisation to the rest of the board. "We're going to operate this year under this philosophy in anything that we do or think about," I said. That can be a tough sell to a room full of CPAs, but I think that by the end of my term, they all had a sense of the power of improv.

In his book *Start with Why*, Simon Sinek says successful leaders all have a "why." Why are they doing what they do? For example, the Apple leadership's "why" is to challenge the status quo. My "why" is to change the conversation to recognize the importance of improvisation.

In the accounting world, we need more than just technical skills. We need interpersonal skills to become better at our jobs to be the best communicators and leaders possible. Younger CPAs often are not developing those skills. I did a course on writing and public presentation at a firm and found that only two people there had a public speaking class in their college curriculum. Nor had business writing been offered.

As leaders, we need to do a better job of that. We need to make our profession look good. We can do that by developing the people who will be making the changes. That's my "why."

I offer a course that I call "How to Dump SALY" (an acronym for "same as last year"). We tend to do things the same way we did last year because, in some cases, it's just the easiest. But we need to dump SALY and find new, creative ways of doing things. SALY is an inherent risk in our profession.

If you have been doing things with clients or customers the same way for a long time, you face a hidden risk, and it could be explosive. It could bring down a company. If you are not thinking and asking the right questions and coming up with creative approaches, you could shut yourself down.

I've repeatedly emphasized throughout this book the power of "yes, and…" They are words of agreement, not conflict. They are words that explore possibilities, not ones that dash hopes. They are about managing stress and not letting it defeat you.

Improvisation Empowerment

Successful leaders are able to focus and immerse themselves in the moment. They can think on their feet and adapt to changing situations. By adopting a "yes, and…" attitude, they become more motivating and inspiring. The respect that such leaders show to others makes them better negotiators. They listen to understand, not just to respond, and as their colleagues feel their support and trust, they produce better results.

These are the kind of leaders who know the difference between being critical and being curious—and that, fundamentally, is how "yes, but..." differs from "yes, and..." The former attacks and tears down. The latter carries the power to convince others that they are wrong, but the approach is far different. It is accepting and respectful of the difference of opinion and seeks to build upon it. It is collegial rather than confrontational.

When you say "yes, but...," you're trying to impose your argument. You're trying to get your way. You're trying to make your point known. When you say "yes, and...," you're still trying to make your point known, but you're also trying to work with others to see what additional points might develop.

As you can see, improvisation is the mark of leadership. Once you understand that, the effect is transformative. Improv can be funny, but it works in situations that aren't very fun at all, regarding matters that could flare into confrontation if handled the wrong way. If you apply these principles, you promote healing and growth instead.

Chapter 9 Takeaways

➪ Dump SALY.

➪ Use the principles of improvisation to strengthen your leadership abilities.

➪ "Yes, and—Yes, and—Yes, and"

As Nike says—Just do it!

Getting the Pieces in Place

Some years ago a friend and I started a business called The Group Mind. We had some large cards printed with the words "Yes, and" on the outside. You opened the card to see: "There are gems in every idea. Embrace and build, and someday one of those ideas will change the world."

I send out those cards as follow-ups and thank-yous. I want people to remember me. We all desire that, and I still wonder how much influence I have on others. After they go home, will they recall three major points that I made in my presentation? Or will I become "that Pete Martini or something guy"?

Ideas indeed have the potential to shake the world. People have told me they still have those cards on their desk so they will always remember to ponder and practice the power of ideas. "Virtues are formed in man by his doing the actions," Aristotle wrote. Excellence is a habit.

If you want to change things, you have to flex that creative muscle. You need to employ improv until it becomes second nature. You have to put it into constant practice to the point where you can't stop doing it. You will believe in yourself and your abilities, and that confidence will propel you to even greater excellence. A golfer understands that principle well: a confident swing produces results. That's what I'm trying to create, a habit and a belief.

"This is too simple, Pete," people sometimes tell me, and I agree. It is simple. It's supposed to be simple. The most powerful concepts are not all that difficult to grasp. You can use improvisation and "yes, and…" in your workplace, your marriage and family, and your relationships—it works at all levels. Each day of our lives is an exercise in improvisation.

After I deliver presentations, I often hear back from those who hire me that they found me easy to work with and that I was adaptable to their needs. I bring it all back to improv. Treat others well, and keep your focus during confusion or crisis. Devote your attention to the person with whom you are speaking. If someone is telling you their needs, listen attentively. If you are just waiting for an opening to make your pitch, it will be readily apparent.

The elements of improvisation—trusting, supporting, respecting, listening, focusing, and adapting, along with "yes, and…"—when working together, will go far to enhance your ability to adapt quickly and appropriately. It's a matter of attitude, and each day we need to strive to get those pieces in place.

Whether you are dealing with issues of career or family, the power of improv will help to get you through. You can move forward with confidence and hope rather than sinking into negativity. These are the principles for effective living and leadership, and success awaits those who embrace them.

CPSIA information can be obtained
at www.ICGtesting.com
Printed in the USA
FSOW03n0947220916
25268FS